D0810899

OLYMPIC CONTROVERSIES

THE IMPORTANT THING IN
THE OLYMPIC GAMES IS NOT
WINNING BUT TAKING PART.
THE ESSENTIAL THING IN
LIFE IS NOT CONQUERING
BUT FIGHTING WELL.

BARON de COUBERTIN.

OLYMPIC CONTROVERSIES

BY HARVEY FROMMER

13769
FRANKLIN WATTS
NEW YORK/LONDON/TORONTO/SYDNEY/1987

Photographs courtesy of: The Bettmann Archive: pp. 2 and 42 (BBC Hulton), 11, 13, 15, 20, 23, 34, 45 (top), 48; New York Public Library Picture Collection: pp. 17, 32, 47, 52, 57, 77; UPI/Bettmann Newsphotos: pp. 37, 54, 61, 66, 87, 90, 92, 106, 115, 117; Springer/Bettmann Film Archive: p. 45 (bottom); AP/Wide World Photos: pp. 58, 74, 94, 101.

Library of Congress Cataloging in Publication Data

Frommer, Harvey.
Olympic controversies.

(An Impact book)
Bibliography: p.
Includes index.
Summary: A history of the Olympic games focusing on the political events, controversies, and tragedies that have marred the games.
1. Olympic games—History—Juvenile literature.
2. Olympic games—Political aspects—Juvenile literature. [1. Olympic games—History]   I. Title.
GV721.5.F76   1987   796.4'8   87-10678
ISBN 0-531-10417-6

CONTENTS

For my family

The important thing in the Olympic Games is not to win but to take part; the important thing in life is not the triumph but the struggle. The essential thing is not to have conquered but to have fought well. To spread these precepts is to build up a stronger and more valiant and, above all, more scrupulous and more gracious humanity.

Baron Pierre de Coubertin

1
INTRODUCTION:
FROM ANCIENT GAMES
TO MODERN OLYMPICS

Almost three thousand years ago in Greece a dozen finalists in a running competition lined up on a 200-yard (183 meters) track. There they competed for the title of the fastest man in the world.

Sprints took place over a distance of one "stade"— 200–210 yards (183–192 meters), about the length of a stadium. There was also the "diaulus," a two-stade race over the course, past pillars of stone, and back again. The long-distance race was seven times twenty-four stades. These footraces made up the prime events of the original Olympic Games together with the five-skill events of the pentathlon: running, leaping, discus, javelin throwing, and wrestling.

The victory ceremony was highly unique. Blaring trumpets sounded as jubilant winners were paraded before the Hellanodikal tribunal. Then the victors were given the highest of honors—a crown of wreaths of wild olive from the sacred grove of Zeus. The victorious athletes became lifetime heroes—exempt from taxes, provided with free feasts for months, and with a splendid statue erected for all to admire.

Through the centuries thousands of these stone statues honored Olympic heroes. Many of them were set in Olympia (a valley area in Greece); others were placed in the main marketplace of the athlete's home town or village.

The ancient Olympic Games, according to one legend, were founded by Hercules, son of the god Zeus, to celebrate his great skills. Another legend claims that the two mighty Greek gods—Zeus and Cronus—battled on the hills above Olympia. The games and religious ceremonies that followed in the valley were organized as a tribute to the victory of Zeus. Still another theory is that the games were a way of honoring Hercules.

Whatever the real origin, the games were a much-prized and significant part of Greek culture and life. Held every four years at holy Olympia in a peaceful valley close by the Altis, the forest shrine of Zeus, the Olympic Games attracted more than forty thousand spectators. They drank wine, slept on the ground, conducted their worship, and cheered on the athletes. Women, however, were barred from the Olympics as either participants or spectators.

Although wars raged and political disputes erupted, although rulers came and went, the Olympic Games continued, from the first recorded one in 776 B.C. to A.D. 393. Through 1,200 years and 320 individual stagings, the games persisted. No single ceremonial event in all of history has ever lasted so long.

In 146 B.C., Roman conquerors took away the freedom of the Greeks. The games were transformed into a disgust-

Above: Olympia. The original home of the Olympic Games. Right: the Ancient Olympics were an important part of Greek culture, as shown in this portrayal of an ancient Greek footrace painted on an antique vase.

ing slaughterhouse in which slaves were performers. In A.D. 394 the Olympics were abolished, and in the centuries that followed even Olympia was destroyed. However, the memory and the message of the Olympic Games remained.

THE FLAME REKINDLED

Not until 1896 did the Olympic spirit return to the world to stay, and for the first time in fourteen centuries, olive branches were awarded to winning athletes. Behind this rebirth of the Olympics was the determination of one man, Pierre de Coubertin, a French aristocrat, scholar, and educator.

In 1887, while on a visit to England, the twenty-four-year-old de Coubertin saw English university students competing in sports. Not only did he think that athletics could be a worthwhile part of an all-round educational program, but he also became obsessed with the idea that would be the focus of his life's work—to revive the ancient Olympic Games that had been staged in Greece and to invite athletes from around the world to compete. His reasoning was that competition in sports would lead to new international friendship and better cooperation among nations. He argued that such games would also expose athletes to people with different values from their own.

In Paris in 1894 at the International Congress of Paris for the Re-establishment of the Olympic Games, seventy-nine delegates from a dozen countries met at Baron de Coubertin's invitation to shape the framework for the new Olympic Games. Agreement was reached on five basic principles: the games would be held every four years, as were the ancient Greek games; contests would be modern

Baron Pierre de Coubertin

12

and not copy the sports of the ancient games; competition would be limited to adults (adult *males* was the understanding); only amateurs would be allowed to take part in the games; and the Olympics would move from city to city every fourth year.

An International Olympic Committee (IOC) was formed in 1896, headed by Baron de Coubertin, who was given the title of Secretary. He selected the majority of the original members of the IOC, and he remained in charge of the IOC until 1925, when he retired.

I SUMMER OLYMPIAD, 1896

In 1896, the first modern Olympics were staged in Athens, Greece. The games began humbly; although amateur athletes from all over the world were invited, only thirteen nations competed: Australia, Austria, Bulgaria, Chile, Denmark, England, France, Germany, Greece, Hungary, Sweden, Switzerland, and the United States. About three hundred athletes traveled to Greece to compete along with two hundred Greeks. None of the nations organized formal teams. Most athletes came to Athens at their own expense. The United States, for example, was represented by athletes from the Boston Athletic Association and Princeton University and one participant from Harvard. Ten sports and forty-three events were on the program, including track and field, the marathon, gymnastics, fencing, cycling, a 100-meter swimming race, lawn tennis, and target shooting.

Americans dominated the track and field events, winning nine of the twelve contests. The first Olympic gold medal winner was James B. Connolly, who won the triple

Crowds entering the stadium to watch the first modern Olympics

jump. Actually, only the first and second winner in an event received prizes: a diploma, a silver medal, and a crown of olive branches for first place; a diploma, a bronze medal, and a crown of laurel for second place. However, all competitors were awarded commemorative medals.

Disappointed Greek fans had little to cheer about until the running of the marathon, which was won by Spirdon Loues, an unknown Greek peasant shepherd from a little village. It was the first international race he had ever run—and the last one. That moment gave Loues lifelong fame. King George I of Greece asked him what he would like as a gift. The marathon victor asked for a horse and cart to carry water.

Pierre de Coubertin's dream—an athlete-centered Olympics with competition for the joy of competition—was a fine one. However, even in the first modern Olympics the seeds of the problems and controversies of the future were in evidence. The Greek royal family used the games as a device to build up its power. The practice of the raising of the national flags of the winning athletes in a victory celebration was put in place.

At a breakfast ceremony on the final Sunday before the end of the games, the king of Greece toasted his nation: "the mother and nurse of the Olympic Games in antiquity." The king then went on to propose that "Athens become the stable and permanent seat of the Olympic Games." American athletes signed a petition agreeing with the king that Athens become the permanent site of all future Olympic Games.

Baron de Coubertin ignored the king's words and the petition. His mind was set on keeping the games "ambula-

Spirdon Loues of Greece, the first
modern Olympic marathon champion

16

tory," and he already was planning for the 1900 games in Paris.

One can only wonder what might have happened if Athens had been selected as a permanent Olympic site. Hindsight shows that some problems, especially the two boycotts in 1980 and 1984 by the United States and the Soviet Union, respectively, would have been avoided.

2
OVERVIEW:
CONTINUING CONTROVERSIES

Every four years the start of the Olympic Games is antici-
pated with the highest intentions on the part of the International Olympic Committee (IOC) and the participants.
Still, every four years recurring problems and issues arise
to create strife and controversy. These problems fall into
several categories. The following are some of the controversies that have affected the Olympics.

CEREMONIES

When Baron de Coubertin revived the games in 1896, he
was very aware that ceremony would add to the atmosphere
of the Olympics. Thus, even from the days of the first
Olympics a certain degree of ritual has always characterized
the games.

The opening ceremony has become bigger and grander
through the years. It has thrilled millions but has also caused
problems. Countries have used it as a way to show off their
national pride. Some teams have competed with each other

Opening ceremony for the 1936 Winter Games.
Over the years, these ceremonies have been
increasingly wrought with political controversy.

to prove who has the best or the most expensive uniforms. Some host nations have used the opening ceremony as a forum to publicize their accomplishments and stature in the world.

In the opening ceremony competitors and officials parade behind their flag and a banner bearing their country's name. Disputes and controversy sometimes result from this; some nations do not recognize other nations.

The oath taken by athletes, judges, and officials is also part of the opening ceremony:

> In the name of all the competitors I promise that I shall take part in these Olympic Games, respecting and abiding by the rules which govern them, in the true spirit of sportsmanship, for the glory of sport and for the honor of our teams.

The oath expresses a worthy ideal, but sometimes the meaning of the oath is lost in the frenzy of competition. Fights between competitors, harsh words exchanged, and bragging boasts have created problems throughout many Olympics.

Victory ceremonies have also been a cause of controversy. Medals are awarded by the president of the IOC or his deputy, plus the president of the International Sport Federation for the event in which the medal was achieved. Popular opinion to the contrary, the medals are not gold but gilded (only overlaid with a thin covering of gold). When they are presented and the national flag of the winner is raised and the national anthem is played, it sometimes seems from the commotion that a nation has won rather than an athlete.

Politics also become a factor in the recording and publicizing of the medal point totals. Medal winning has become a way of saying that one political system or nation is superior to another.

Sometimes even the playing of a national anthem or the raising of a country's flag causes problems. As governments change, so do the symbols and the songs of those governments. Many disputes have arisen when the wrong anthem was played or the incorrect flag was raised, even though national Olympic committees are charged with the responsibility to indicate their choices.

TELEVISION

The Berlin Olympics of 1936 marked the first time that television transmitted the games. Audiences of a few thousand viewed athletic and swimming events in halls in Berlin and a few other cities in Germany.

The first time television pictures of the games were transmitted from one nation to another was in 1960 in Rome. The 1964 Winter Games in Innsbruck, Austria, and the Summer Games in Tokyo further intensified television coverage. The games in Tokyo were the first ones relayed via satellite from one continent to another.

The images shown on television helped transform Austria, particularly Innsbruck, into a major sports center and tourist attraction. Television coverage of the games at Innsbruck was also used to promote sales of Austrian ski equipment.

Television transmission of the Tokyo Games helped transform Japan into one of the top trading nations in the world. "Without the Olympics," the mayor of Tokyo said, "Japan would not have risen to its high position in world trade so fast."

In 1976 equipment costing 100 million dollars transmitted pictures of the Montreal Olympics via satellite around the world each day to audiences of over 800 million. ABC-TV paid 25 million dollars for the rights to televise the Montreal Olympics.

The Los Angeles Olympics of 1984 boasted a television audience that was the largest in the history of the

A cameraman captures the festivities of 6,000 athletes marching in Wembley Stadium, London, during the opening of the 1948 Summer Olympics.

world. ABC-TV paid 225 million dollars for the American rights, but the network truly got its money's worth. ABC's publicity as a television sports network enabled it to earn much money from the advertising rates charged to sponsors.

It is clear that Olympic popularity has been tremendously influenced by television, and television has tremendously influenced the Olympics. Starting and ending times of events—in fact, all scheduling—has been worked out with television in mind. The opening and closing ceremonies have become television extravaganzas. Space has become a logistical problem for host nations, who have to find the room to house an army of television journalists and technicians plus ever increasing amounts of equipment. Competitors in many events wear numbers not only on the fronts and backs of their uniforms but also on the sides of their shorts to provide ease of television identification.

With television's all-seeing eye on the scene all of the grace and power and speed of the Olympics have come to a watching world. So too have controversy and tragedy: the Black Power salutes of a pair of U.S. track stars in Mexico City, various demonstrations, and the terrorists who massacred members of the Israeli Olympic team in 1972.

DRUGS

Drugs in the world of sports continually create controversy, and the Olympic scene has not been exempt. Some Olympic athletes have been accused of using steroids and other drugs to enhance their sports performance and to gain an unfair advantage over their competitors. Several athletes who have allegedly used drugs have been barred from Olympic competition. And although drug testing of individuals has been much debated as an invasion of individual privacy, it is now a permanent part of the Olympic scene.

24

COMMERCIALISM

The Olympic amateur spirit of sport for the sake of sport has become more and more commercialized through the years. For some, the pursuit of Olympic gold has given way to the race for real gold.

In the 1960s endorsement of sports products by athletes set off argument and debate. European skiers, for example, used equipment that clearly displayed the logo or name of the manufacturer. In return, cash payments and other forms of compensation were given to skiers and other athletes, who at times resembled walking billboards.

Adidas and Puma, two sports equipment manufacturers, reportedly paid track and field athletes to wear their shoes during competition in the 1968 Summer Olympics. An investigation was held, and findings revealed that it was common practice for various manufacturers to pay athletes to "sport" their equipment.

"Most of us are aware that as many as two-thirds of the athletes signing the Olympic oath are committing perjury," observed Jack Kelly, president of the Amateur Athletic Union.

The problems of commercialism forced the IOC to modify its rigid rules in 1974. Amateur athletes, while in training for international competition and not at work, were allowed to receive their regular salaries from their employers. It was a form of athletic leave of absence.

Additionally, the IOC ruled that open endorsement of a product by an athlete was allowed. However, the fee for the endorsement had to be paid to the national sport organization the athlete belonged to. The national sport group was then permitted to give expense money to the athlete.

Charismatic, record-breaking, and medal-winning athletes have found the Olympics to be a path not only to glory but to riches. Past Olympians like Johnny Weissmuller,

Sonja Henie, and Babe Didrikson cashed in commercially on their accomplishments. However, they never dreamed of what contemporary heroes would achieve commercially.

Mark Spitz, who racked up seven gold medals in the 1972 games in Munich, became an advertiser's dream. He allegedly received 5 million dollars in fees to endorse all kinds of products. Bruce Jenner, Montreal Games decathlon champ, made no secret of his commercial desires. Jenner said he put himself through the most difficult training routines knowing they would pay off for him commercially. They did. Jenner and his wife became super-sellers for breakfast cereals, cameras, clothing—all types of goods and services.

Eric Heiden won five gold medals in speed skating at Lake Placid in 1980. Offered various commercial endorsements, he turned them down. Heiden explained that he did not wish to commercialize his Olympic accomplishments.

However, for every Eric Heiden there have been dozens of commercially minded performers like Mary Lou Retton, Frank Shorter, Dorothy Hamill, and the U.S. gold medal-winning hockey team of 1980.

Six of the American hockey team gold medalists managed to sign contracts with National Hockey League teams for salaries of about one hundred thousand dollars a season. Goalie Jim Craig received a forty-five-thousand-dollar bonus and signed a three-year deal with the Atlanta Flames at eighty-five thousand dollars a year. Craig also was given legal assurances of commercial endorsements. For a one-minute Coca-Cola commercial on television he was paid thirty-five thousand dollars.

Manufacturers have learned that it is smart business to associate themselves with the Olympics. Thus, for a fee, companies have been able to become the "Official Olympic" beer, camera, car, book, soda, sweat suit, typewriter, sneaker, film, watch, and so on.

It has become a two-way commercial street. Sponsors pay large sums of money to the IOC, the local organizing groups, and the national committees; in return the sponsors receive the right to be "official."

In sum, the greatest amateur competition in the world is still that—with a lot of commercialism thrown in. Controversy will always revolve around these questions: How much commercialism can the Olympics tolerate and how much commercialism can be eliminated while still allowing the games to survive, given the mounting costs of staging the event?

Then there are the many controversies that have occurred in specific Olympic Games and events and also in certain periods of history. These controversies over the years have had a major impact on the history of these celebrated games.

3
THE OLYMPICS FROM
1900 TO WORLD WAR I

From the turn of the twentieth century to the advent of World War I, the four Olympiads (an Olympiad being a measurement of time equal to four years) held during this period developed from games marred by confusion and mockery to games filled with excitement, gaining increasing popularity and respect.

II SUMMER OLYMPIAD, 1900

The Olympic Games of 1900, held in Paris in honor of Baron de Coubertin, witnessed competition by 1,139 athletes, including 11 women, from twenty-two nations. It was a dramatic increase in the number of participants. However, although there were more athletes in Paris, there were also more problems for the Olympic movement.

The opening ceremony was scheduled for a Sunday, and American athletes refused to take part. The date was switched to July 14, a Saturday, which was Bastille Day, a major holiday in France. This caused more problems. The

28

actual athletic competition began the next day—a Sunday—and again many Americans refused to compete. Their behavior resulted in strained relations between the United States and France.

Baron de Coubertin had looked on the Paris Olympics as a part of the 1900 Paris Exposition, but French governmental officials lacked his enthusiasm for athletics and did not offer much cooperation. Coordination of events caused major political battles.

Since the playing facilities were scattered all over Paris, problems developed in the transportation of athletes and spectators, causing some journalists to ignore certain events because of the difficulties of getting to the competition sites.

The games themselves were a muddled, odd-lot assortment of sports. Some of the competitions were officially recognized; other events were billed as exhibitions. Still others were just there. World amateur championship matches vied with world professional matches.

A rugby football match was staged at Vincennes, a suburb of Paris. The entire affair was a mob scene, with police straining to keep things under control. Defeated in the Franco-Prussian War by the Germans, the French sought revenge in the rugby match. They were able to achieve what they desired—defeating Germany 25 to 16, according to some newspapers, or by 27 to 17, according to other reports. Olympic record keeping was not a model of efficiency at the Paris Games.

Confusion held center stage. Reference books cite yachting results as official; they were not. Association football, rugby, and polo are listed as names of events in official programs. According to published data, however, the only official events were cricket, croquet, and golf. But this was not the case. Staples of the Olympics like boxing, wrestling, and weight lifting were oddly enough not even a part of the Paris Games.

In truth, the Paris Games were poorly run, but many

of the athletes were outstanding. A few women made a triumphant entry into the Olympics, and Charlotte Cooper of Great Britain won the women's singles lawn tennis tournament to earn a place in history as the first woman Olympic champion.

Purdue University's 6-foot 5-inch (197 cm), spider-legged Ray Ewry won three gold medals in the standing high jump, standing long jump, and standing triple jump. The mainly French audience was astounded at the exploits of the American with the 40-inch (100-centimeter) leg length. Ewry stood motionless as a statue and jumped horizontally 11 feet (338 cm), stood perfectly still and leaped straight up 5½ feet (169 cm) into the air. Other outstanding feats were accomplished by athletes from the University of Pennsylvania, who shattered eleven world records in track and field.

When the Paris Games finally came to a close, it was clear that they had been viewed by many as mainly a sideshow to the Paris Exposition. Pierre de Coubertin, his name not mentioned even once by journalists, was sadly lost in the shuffle. And even the eager and ambitious baron finally had to comment about the Paris Olympics: "There was much goodwill but the interesting results had nothing Olympic about them. We have made a hash of our work."

III SUMMER OLYMPIAD, 1904

In 1904 St. Louis was the site of the first Olympics staged in the United States. Held in conjunction with the Louisiana Purchase Exposition (World's Fair), the games had an ambitious program of events: boxing, wrestling, fencing, weight lifting, rowing, a full schedule of swimming events, a complete gymnastics program, and lawn tennis.

However, like the second Olympics, the St. Louis Games were also a disappointment. The voyage from Europe by steamship and then by train or riverboat to St. Louis posed problems for Europeans. Only twelve nations were represented in the third modern Olympics. In all, there were 617 competitors, but travel difficulties gave the athletic delegation a North American flavor. More than five hundred athletes were from the United States, and forty-one were Canadian. France sent no athletic delegation.

Track and field events were held on the beautiful campus of Washington University, but other competitions were staged amid the carnival atmosphere of the world's fair. Once again the Olympics were a kind of sideshow to another event. This created anger and disgust on the part of some of the foreign delegations.

"I was not only present at a sporting contest," said a Hungarian, "but also at a fair where there were sports, where there was cheating, where monsters were exhibited for a joke."

A low point in Olympic competition took place at the end of the marathon run. Fred Lorz of the United States entered the stadium to the wild cheers of the crowd. Later it was learned that Lorz had hitched a car ride to help him overcome fatigue. "I only did it as a joke," explained Lorz.

Because of the action of Lorz and the atmosphere at the games, many looked on the Olympics as a farce. And the staging of "Anthropological Days" did not help the image of the games. Pygmies, Sioux, Kaffirs, Ainu, and other tribesmen competed against each other in events such as bow-and-arrow shooting, pole climbing, and mud fighting.

Despite the circus-like atmosphere that attached itself to the third Olympic Games in St. Louis, the dream of a true international sports competition still remained. Baron de Coubertin maintained to all those who would listen that the Olympics would become the greatest sports event in history.

IV SUMMER OLYMPIAD, 1908

The games of the IV Olympiad were held in London in 1908. With the most athletes (2,059), the most spectators,

*Cartoon depicting Fred Lorz taking a
break from the marathon race to watch
the competition and get some help from
a car to finish the race*

the most countries (twenty-two), and the most expertly managed Olympics to that point in time, the London Games were a huge success in many ways. Women took part in the archery competition, as they had in 1904, and in a gymnastic exhibition; ice skating was added to the Olympic program for the first time.

"We saw," announced King Edward VII, who presided over it all, "the jolliest best show on earth."

It might have been the jolliest show, but it also was one beset by problems. In the opening ceremonies British officials somehow neglected to display the American flag along with those of other nations. The lame excuse was that they had been unable to locate an American flag. Athletes from the United States carried small American flags as they marched past the reviewing stand presided over by King Edward VII and Queen Alexandra. The American standard-bearer, Martin Sheridan, refused to lower the U.S. flag.

"This flag," Sheridan was reported to have said, "dips to no earthly king." The tradition of not dipping the American flag still exists.

Disagreements involving other flags took place at the London Games. The delegation from Finland was told it was to carry a Russian flag, and the Finns retaliated by carrying no flag at all. Soviet and Finnish athletes almost came to blows. Irish athletes were angry because they were required to march under the flag of Great Britain.

Reggie Walker, a South African schoolboy, won the 100-meter dash in record time, while Britain's Henry Taylor won the 400-meter and 1,500-meter freestyle swimming.

One of the most dramatic moments took place when Dorando Pietri, a candy maker from Italy, stumbled into the stadium in the final lap of the marathon. Turning the wrong way, he spun and fell down. Officials pushed him along toward the finish line. After he fell four times, the half-dead runner was practically carried across the finish line by fans and others. British officials announced that Pietri had won the marathon, but after some debating Pietri's

33

*Officials help Dorando Pietri to the
finish line. He was later disqualified.*

victory was disallowed. Hayes, an American, was declared the winner of the marathon.

Although many individual athletic highlights marked the London Olympics, there were quite a few controversies on the field of competition, especially between the British and American teams.

What became known as the "Battle of Shepherd's Bush" began when American John Carpenter was disqualified in the 400-meter race for fouling Scotsman Wyndham Halswelle. The race was ordered to be rerun. All of the American runners protested and refused to compete. And Halswelle became the first and only man in the history of the Olympics to compete against no opponents.

When the London Games ended, various nations claimed victory on a per-capita basis. And there was more squabbling. Some critics continued to wonder if the Olympics were such a good idea.

V SUMMER OLYMPIAD, 1912

Stockholm was the setting for the 1912 Olympics, and the V Olympic Games rescued the Olympic movement from the poor planning and poor sportsmanship of earlier meetings. They were the most exciting and star-studded games seen up to that point. Twenty-eight nations (including Japan and China for the first time) and 2,541 athletes competed in a magnificent new stadium of gray-violet native brick.

American newspapers became truly interested in the Olympics for the first time; stories about the games became front-page news. Also, electronic timing was employed for the first time. Previously active in only gymnastics and figure skating, women competed in a couple of swimming events.

Jim Thorpe, an American Indian, was the winner in both the five-event pentathlon and the ten-event decathlon (each made up of track and field events) and became the first international hero in sports. His performance was an amazing exhibition of power, endurance, and grace. Granted a personal audience with Sweden's King Gustav V, who complimented him on his ability, Thorpe responded with these words: "Thanks, King."

Beachboy Duke Kahanamoku of Hawaii was trailed by hundreds of fanatic admirers. The duke won the 100-meter freestyle gold medal and set a world record. Hannes Kolehminen of Finland amazed everyone with his endurance. Hannes "the Mighty" won the grueling 5,000-meter and 10,000-meter races as well as the cross-country race.

The dream of Baron Pierre de Coubertin—peaceful competition—seemed to have been realized. The problems, predicaments, and controversies of the past paled beside the potential of the future shown by the Stockholm Games.

Just six months later, while the glow of the splendid Stockholm Olympics was still in the public mind, controversy once again surfaced. Jim Thorpe, who had been called by King Gustav of Sweden "the most wonderful athlete in the world," was charged with violation of the amateur code by the Amateur Athletic Union (AAU). An American sportswriter reported that Thorpe had earlier played minor league baseball for a Rocky Mount, North Carolina, team.

"I did not play for the money," Thorpe said. The money was meager. "I played because I liked baseball."

Jack Thorpe, son of legendary American Indian athlete, Jim Thorpe, holds up one of his father's Olympic gold medals that were returned to Thorpe's children by the International Olympic Committee. A picture of Jim Thorpe can be seen in the background.

The AAU took away Thorpe's amateur status; the International Olympic Committee then stripped Thorpe of his Olympic medals, claiming he had violated the amateur code. These actions set off a chain of debates all over the world concerning the amateur policies of the Olympics and what many thought was harsh and shameful treatment of one of the greatest athletes in the history of the world. And it was not until 1983—twenty-one years after Thorpe's death—that his medals were returned to his family and his marks reinstated.

4
THE OLYMPICS BETWEEN
TWO WORLD WARS
(1920-1936)

While world war was avoided for nearly two decades, the Olympic Games of those years established many precedents. The Olympic flag, the Olympic slogan, and the Olympic Village were all introduced; women began competing in their own separate events; and for the first time there were Winter Olympics. These and other innovations set the foundation for better organized and more international Olympics.

VII SUMMER OLYMPIAD, 1920

The sixth modern Olympics were scheduled for Berlin in 1916 and viewed by Baron de Coubertin as an undertaking of "gladness and concord." Instead World War I took center stage and the games were cancelled. More than 10 million men died in mortal combat; an equal number were maimed and wounded in battle. The playing fields of Europe became areas of shell craters, barbed wire, and devastation. The war raged for four long years, and when it ended, many also predicted the end of the Olympic Games.

However, a last-minute decision was made by the Olympic committee to stage the VII Olympiad in Antwerp, Belgium. Ravaged by the war, the tiny nation of Belgium built facilities quickly, even though many were makeshift. The games went on in a small school stadium that was restructured for the event. Only twenty-nine nations and fewer than three thousand athletes competed. Germany, Austria, Hungary, and Turkey—losers in the war—were excluded from participation by the International Olympic Committee (IOC).

Several innovations introduced at the Antwerp Games became part of the Olympics. In an attempt to heal the wounds of World War I, a mass prayer for humanity opened the VII Olympiad. The five-ringed Olympic flag was also introduced. The five linked rings symbolize the five continents of the world and include the national colors of practically all of the Olympic-world countries. The Antwerp Games also saw the introduction of the Olympic slogan: *Citius, Altius, Fortius* (Faster, Higher, Stronger).

The U.S. team sent to Antwerp was composed mainly of ex-servicemen. The 351 athletes traveled to the games on the *Princess Matoika*, a military transport ship employed during World War I to bring the dead back to the United States from France and Germany. The morbid quality of the passage to Belgium and the living conditions in Antwerp played havoc with the morale of the Americans.

One athlete was dismissed from the team for failing to make a curfew in the abandoned schoolhouse that was the barracks for the U.S. team. Almost two hundred American athletes signed a petition demanding that the U.S. Olympic Committee reinstate him. After much bickering their request was honored, but the incident set the mood of bitterness that lingered over American athletes throughout the Antwerp Games.

Olympic highlights included a French runner, an Italian walker, and the U.S. crew team. Joseph Guillemot of France, his lungs badly damaged in a gas attack during the war, barely hung on to defeat the great Paavo Nurmi in the 5,000 meters. Ugo Frigerio of Italy heeled and toed his way around the stadium to win both walking races. Frigerio waved wildly to the spectators and was his own cheerleader, with shouts of "Viva! Viva!" to himself. The powerful U.S. Naval Academy's eight-oar crew finished first to trigger a string of eight consecutive triumphs for the United States in that event.

The significance of the Antwerp Games was to show that not even a world war, lasting longer than the period of a whole Olympiad, could stop or weaken the Olympic movement. In fact, the Olympics were stronger than ever.

I WINTER OLYMPIAD, 1924

Until 1924 there had been no Winter Olympic Games. Although Baron de Coubertin was opposed to the staging of separate Winter Olympics, winter sports were very popular in Europe, and there was pressure to make them part of the Olympics. In 1924 Winter Games were staged in Chamonix, France, on an experimental basis. Competition took place in five sports: skiing, figure skating, ice hockey, speed skating, and bobsledding. Sixteen nations represented by 293 athletes took part, and the Winter Games were a great success despite too much snow and rain. The first major hero of Olympic winter sports was Thorlief Haug of Norway, winner of three gold medals in the 18-kilometer and 50-kilometer cross-country skiing events and the Nordic combined—cross country and ski jump.

VIII SUMMER OLYMPIAD, 1924

The Summer Olympics of 1924 in Paris had their share of heroes too. The style and substance of the games were immortalized in the fine 1981 film *Chariots of Fire*. However, contrary to the serene setting shown in the movie,

Paris was not that perfect an environment for Olympic competition.

Prior to the games the Seine River overflowed its banks and flooded the city. The area of Colombes was swelteringly hot; temperatures reached as high as 113 degrees. Fans suffered from the intense heat, and some fainted and had to be taken to hospitals. Despite these environmental problems, the 1924 Olympics proved that the games had become big business. Scalpers made huge profits selling tickets. And major cities all over the world started to get in on the bidding, hoping to be selected as the next site for the games.

Political considerations influenced the 1924 Olympics. Germany and her World War I allies were once again excluded from participation. Russia, which had undergone a communist revolution, was not welcome.

Women also were not welcome as Olympic competitors by Pierre de Coubertin. He had consistently excluded them from participation in track and field and only grudgingly allowed them to compete in golf and tennis in 1900 and in a few events in 1912.

European women led the protests for full participation by female athletes in the Olympics. In 1920 Baron de Coubertin fought off a challenge by women who wished to compete fully in the games. The First Women's Olympic Games were staged in Paris in 1922. This proved to be the wedge that convinced the IOC to override de Coubertin's objections to women's Olympic involvement.

Women in the United States were discouraged from competing in international sports events by female physical educators, who argued that participation would be too

A ski jumper competing in the first Winter Olympic Games, held in 1924 in Chamonix, France

rigorous. Despite this attitude two American women athletes—Gertrude Ederle in 1924 and Mildred "Babe" Zaharias in 1932—went on to become major Olympic stars.

The high athletic drama at the 1924 Olympics was focused on track and field events, which saw large numbers of contestants competing. Nearly fifteen hundred athletes from forty-four nations took part in these events alone. One ship arrived in Paris carrying a U.S. squad that numbered 320 including officials. U.S. Navy officials came on their own ship.

Although American athletes distinguished themselves at the games of the VIII Olympiad, it was the competitors from other nations who became immortal. Britain's Eric Liddell in the 400 meters and Harold Abrahams in the 100 meters captured the fancy and the respect of the world. Paavo Nurmi of Finland, carrying a stopwatch and running with incredible drive, set a world record in the 10,000 meters and an Olympic record in the 1,500 and 5,000 meters, and he finished first in the 3,000-meter race.

The shy and handsome swimmer Johnny Weissmuller, an authentic American hero then nineteen years old, won the 100- and 400-meter freestyle events, anchored the 800-meter relay team, and performed on the bronze medal-winning water polo team. His splendid performance in Paris popularized swimming in America and made swimmers the equal of track and field performers as athletes.

Weissmuller was celebrated as the greatest swimmer of the first half of the twentieth century. He went on to star as Tarzan in motion pictures. And this set off another debate, which would grow louder in the years ahead: How "commercial" should Olympic athletes become?

II WINTER OLYMPIAD, 1928

The original plan was to stage both the Summer and Winter Games in the same nation during the same calendar year,

Left: Johnny Weissmuller, champion swimmer in both the 1924 and 1928 Olympics. Below: later, he played the popular hero Tarzan in the movies.

but this proved unworkable. In 1928, for example, the Dutch lacked the appropriate facilities for winter sports, so the Winter Olympics were moved to St. Moritz, Switzerland, where more than five hundred athletes representing twenty-five countries competed. The 1928 Olympics witnessed the phenomenon of a woman receiving international sports headlines. At the age of fifteen, Sonja Henie won the first of three straight gold medals. She contributed greatly to the popularity of skating and helped to allay criticism of the role of women in sports. Canada won the hockey championship for the second straight time, but it was Norway that surprisingly edged out the United States in the overall medal standings.

IX SUMMER OLYMPIAD, 1928

Amsterdam remained the site of the Summer Olympics in 1928. These games transformed the Summer Olympics into a truly international contest as a record forty-six nations and three thousand athletes competed. For the first time since World War I, athletes from Germany, Bulgaria, Austria, and Hungary were allowed to compete.

Smaller nations distinguished themselves in the Amsterdam Games in a big way. The soccer title was won by Uruguay, while Argentina and New Zealand won gold medals in boxing. India was the victor in field hockey. Japan won its first gold medals. The hammer throw was won by Ireland. And even the little nation of Haiti won a silver medal.

The 1928 games saw a great step forward for women

A breathtaking view of the ski jump at St. Moritz, with the Swiss Alps in the background

in the Olympic movement and a small step backward too. Women had their own track and field program and expanded swimming events. They competed in team gymnastics but were restricted from competing in individual events.

Eleven women entered the 800-meter race, which cheered supporters of female participation in the Olympics. However, five women dropped out before the race was finished. Another five were drained and exhausted and collapsed after reaching the finish line. The remaining woman competitor finished the race but collapsed in the dressing room after the event. What happened in the 800 meters stirred new controversy about the role of women in the Olympics. The argument that women were incapable of competing in vigorous events was strengthened, and the IOC dropped the 800-meter race for women from future Olympic programs.

The U.S. Olympic team won twenty-two gold medals in the 1928 games to lead all nations, but its track and field delegation was a huge disappointment. The team won only seven medals and was shut out totally in the dashes. The 1928 team was pampered. It was reported that on its voyage to Europe aboard the *S.S. President Roosevelt* the three-hundred-member team ate 580 steaks in a single meal and gorged itself on huge quantities of ice cream.

National pride in Olympic teams became even more accentuated at the Amsterdam Games. The lofty ideal publicly proclaimed by Olympic leaders that taking part in the games was more important than winning was just that—a lofty ideal.

The nationalistic lessons of the 1928 Olympics were expressed by Major Douglas MacArthur, president of the U.S. Olympic Committee: "Nothing is more synonymous of

*Sonja Henie, the
first Olympic heroine*

our national success than is our national success in athletics."
His comment would become an Olympic theme not only
for the United States but for other nations as well. And
unfortunately, this nationalistic view of the games would
lead to excesses in the years ahead and outright mockery
of the Olympic spirit.

III WINTER OLYMPIAD, 1932

In 1932 the United States was to be the site of the Olympics
for the first time in almost thirty years; the United States
would host both the Summer and Winter Games.

The selection of the little-known town of Lake Placid,
New York, as the site of the 1932 Winter Olympic Games
created some controversy. Scandinavian nations objected,
claiming that the United States lacked experience in staging
winter events. Warm weather during the winter competition
further fueled the criticism, and attendance was reduced
because the United States was experiencing the Great Depression. Nevertheless, the 1932 Winter Olympics were
highly successful, especially from the vantage point of U.S.
sports, as American athletes won all four speed skating
medals and were victorious in the two-man and four-man
bobsledding events. Edde Eagan, a member of the triumphant four-man bobsledding team, became the only athlete
in history to win a gold medal in both the Winter and Summer Olympics. Eagan had won a gold in light heavyweight
boxing in 1920.

X SUMMER OLYMPIAD, 1932

In 1932 the world was in the grip of a depression. In California alone more than seven hundred thousand people
were unemployed. The city of Los Angeles—the Olympic

site—was relatively unknown and small compared to previous Olympic sites.

"The games will be a farce," some experts predicted. Others thought that with the world's economy so poor there should not even be an Olympics in 1932. Many nations objected to the expense of traveling great distances to compete in Los Angeles. Just six months before the games were scheduled to start, no nation was firmly committed to competing. Critics notwithstanding, the Los Angeles Games were held, and they proved to be the most successful to that point in Olympic history.

Cooperation and commitment made it all possible. Steamship lines offered reduced rates to national teams, and delegations numbering fifteen hundred athletes from thirty-four nations traveled to California. Some of the teams came at great sacrifice. Brazilians paid their way by making the voyage on a ship loaded with coffee beans, and they sold the beans at port stops on the way to California.

Innovation marked the Los Angeles Games. The Olympic Village—quarters where all athletes live together during the games—was established. The Village concept was the idea of the IOC and its secretary, Zack Farmer, to house and feed athletes for just two dollars a day. It was an idea that literally saved the 1932 Olympics.

The victory stand was another new feature. It provided prestige and publicity for the crowning of winning athletes. Another innovation was electric photo-timing for races, a primitive version of today's methods. The official timing was still by hand, but electric photo-timing was used as a backup. The new method came into use in the 100-meter dash to determine the winner of a race between Americans Eddie Tolan and Ralph Metcalfe who finished just inches apart.

Pomp and circumstance totally characterized the Los Angeles Games and would set a pattern for the future. Ceremonies featured more than thirty bands, the 107-foot-

51

THE IMPORTANT THING IN THE
OLYMPIC GAMES IS NOT WINNING
BUT TAKING PART- THE ESSEN-
TIAL THING IS NOT CONQUERING
BUT FIGHTING WELL
DE COUBERTIN

The opening of the Los Angeles Olympics in 1932.
The Olympic torch sits high above the large crowd.
At the end of the ceremony, hundreds of white
doves were released into the sky, spreading
the Olympic message of peace.

high Olympic torch, a 1,220-voice chorus that sang the *Hymne Olympique*, the boom of 75-millimeter guns, and the high-stepping majorettes.

Critics of Los Angeles as a site for the Olympics had claimed that the city's dry, subtropical climate would reduce attendance and cut down on the quality of athletic performance. The critics were wrong on both counts. On opening day 105,000 spectators crowded into the Memorial Coliseum. Daily attendance there and at the Rose Bowl averaged sixty-five thousand. And more than a million people watched the marathoners run through the streets of the City of Angels.

The Los Angeles Games saw sixteen world records broken, two tied, thirty new Olympic marks set, and a host of new heroes crowned. The first American Olympic heroine emerged—Mildred "Babe" Didrikson, the eighteen-year-old daughter of Norwegian immigrants, shattered the world record in the 80-meter hurdles, the high jump, and the javelin throw. She won two gold medals and would have won more had she been allowed to compete in other events. However, the Olympic rules for 1932 specified that female athletes be allowed to enter only three events. "I'd break all the records," the Babe said, "if they'd only let me." Babe Didrikson, like Johnny Weissmuller before her, went on to great fame after the Olympics, starring in women's basketball and softball, later baseball and tennis, and finally professional golf.

One controversy involved the 3,000-meter steeplechase. Laps were miscounted by officials, and the runners were forced to race an extra 400 meters.

The Los Angeles Games of 1932 attracted more than 1¼ million spectators, and when the final audit was made public, it was disclosed that the Los Angeles Olympic Organizing Committee had managed to create a surplus of almost 1 million dollars.

Some called the Los Angeles Games a Hollywood extravaganza, especially since the style and tone were so

glittering in that depression year. However, the end result was to place Los Angeles on the map as a city of power and prestige. And other cities and states did not miss the message of these games—that the Olympics was a vehicle that publicized and promoted its site as no other sporting event in the world could.

IV WINTER OLYMPIAD, 1936

Like the United States four years earlier, Germany hosted both the Summer and Winter Olympics in 1936. A world on the brink of war was the setting for the Winter Olympic Games in Garmisch-Partenkirchen, Germany. In many nations debate about participating in the games preceded the Winter Olympics of 1936.

More than fifteen thousand attended the opening ceremonies despite a blizzard, while the presence of Adolf Hitler and the masses of Nazi uniformed troops changed the climate of the games into a symbolic stage of the world war to come. A poignant note concerns the great Norwegian ski jumper, Birger Ruud, who successfully defended his title that year: he and his two brothers were later imprisoned in a Nazi concentration camp during World War II.

XI SUMMER OLYMPIAD, 1936

Politics pervaded the atmosphere and polluted the Summer Games of 1936 in Berlin. Civil war in Spain caused that

Babe Didrikson first won fame and popularity as an Olympic track and field star. Later, she became a professional athlete in five different sports.

nation's athletes to return home even before the games began. Brazil sent two teams, each representing a different political viewpoint. Both teams were barred from competing.

The Nazis spent an estimated 30 million dollars, much more money than the total cost of staging all of the previous Olympic Games. Twelve days before the Olympics began, a torch was lit at the sacred altar at Olympia. Carried by more than three thousand runners for about one kilometer each, the torch passed through Greece, Bulgaria, Yugoslavia, Hungary, Austria, and Czechoslovakia.

The torch arrived just at the start of the opening ceremony at Olympic Stadium in Berlin, where 110,000 spectators waited. Thirty trumpets blared over loudspeakers as Adolf Hitler, the head of Nazi Germany, dressed in a dull-brown uniform and the high leather boots of a storm trooper, presided.

Hitler saw the Olympics as a way of making a political statement. He arranged for producer Leni Riefenstahl to make a 7-million-dollar film of the event. That movie, *Olympia*, is still one of the classics of filmmaking and propaganda.

A huge orchestra and chorus were led by aged composer Richard Strauss. *Deutschland über alles* (Germany over all) and a new *Olympic Hymn* written by Strauss were featured. The athletic teams were reviewed by Hitler as they marched in. Cheers greeted the delegations that dipped their colors and saluted Nazi-style. All other athletes were acknowledged only with silence from the huge crowd.

There was the poignancy of a recorded message from a sick and dying Baron Pierre de Coubertin. "The important thing at the Olympic Games," said the frail voice of the father of the modern Olympiad, "is not to win, but to take

*The Olympic torch being
lit for the 1936 Games*

56

*Adolf Hitler presiding over the Olympic Games
in Berlin. He saw the games as a way of
showing off Germany's political and military
power to the rest of the world.*

part, just as the important thing about life is not to conquer but to struggle well."

In contradiction of all that Baron de Coubertin and freedom-loving people stood for, Nazi flags flew from almost every building in Berlin. There were no Nazi flags in the Jewish quarters, for the Nuremberg Laws of 1935 denied Jews permission to display the German flag. Instead, the peaceful Olympic flag of five different-colored rings set on a white background was displayed by Jewish people.

Military organizations had a key role in the running of the Berlin Games, and hundreds of thousands of people were part of the audience that bore witness to that very ceremonious Olympics. Even a festival play that was not part of the games attracted ten thousand people.

Organization and propaganda to improve Germany's image were on parade. News bulletins in five languages were distributed to nearly four thousand newspapers and magazines, almost three thousand of which were published outside Germany. The rooms of journalists suspected of being hostile to Germany were searched. And the Olympic Stadium press box was occupied from time to time by people who were not there to report on the games but to spy on those reporting on the games.

The anti-Semitic and anti-black policies of Nazi leader Adolf Hitler had created controversy in the United States many months before the Olympics began. Avery Brundage, head of the American Olympic Committee (AOC), had urged that the United States participate in the Berlin Games. Like millions of other people, former Judge Jeremiah T. Mahoney, a Catholic and president of the Amateur Athletic Union (AAU), was disgusted with the politics of Nazi Germany and argued for an American boycott by which no American athletes would compete and no American team would be sent to represent the United States.

Brundage claimed that the boycott plan was a Jewish–Communist conspiracy even though a Gallup poll revealed that 57 percent of the American people favored a boycott.

"Jews and Communists," Brundage wrote to a Nazi friend, "threatened to spend a million dollars to keep the United States out of Germany . . . by use of bribery, corruption and political trickery and other contemptible tactics."

At the AAU convention in 1935 Brundage used some trickery of his own and was able to defeat by two and one-half votes a resolution calling for a boycott. Mahoney resigned as AAU president. Brundage succeeded him and became the head of both the AAU and AOC.

The American track and field team contained ten black athletes. German newspapers mocked them, calling them "the black auxiliary" and printing stories that made them appear in a bad light. Cornelius Johnson, a black athlete, posted a record leap in the high jump. Even though Hitler had personally congratulated the first two track and field competition winners, he snubbed Johnson by leaving his box in the stadium.

"It looked as if it was going to rain" was the explanation for Hitler's quick exit given by a spokesman. The real explanation was that Hitler did not want to shake hands with the black American and was upset by Johnson's victory.

The ten blacks on the American track and field team won eight gold medals, three silver medals, and two bronze medals—outscoring every national track and field team including their own fifty-six white teammates.

Jesse Owens, grandson of slaves, born in Alabama, won four gold medals. His most dramatic moment came in a broad-jump duel with blond German Lutz Long. Owens defeated Long and set a world record for the broad jump. Then the white German and the black American walked arm and arm around the giant stadium, astonishing the huge throng. "It took a lot of courage for Long to befriend me in front of Hitler," Owens recalled.

Another political incident took place when two American runners—the only two Jewish ones on the U.S. track and field team—were dropped from the 400-meter relay team at the last moment by coach Dean Cromwell. He

Lutz Long and Jesse Owens

claimed that he was worried about a German victory. It was a poor excuse, for one of the Jewish runners had posted a time equal to that of the runner who replaced him.

Sports fans remember the Olympics in Berlin in 1936 for the achievements of Jesse Owens, who became an instant international hero by winning four gold medals and setting a long-jump record of 26 feet 5¼ inches (813 cm) that would not be broken until 1960.

For others those memorable Berlin Games will always be thought of as the "Nazi Olympics." Storm troopers, flags with swastikas, and the anti-black and anti-Jewish propaganda made a shambles of what should have been the peaceful competition of the Olympics.

An ironic postscript exists to the 1936 games. On the eve of World War II, Hitler had planned the construction of a massive stadium to seat four hundred thousand. His vision was to stage future Olympic Games in that stadium. Athletic competition, in his view, would be confined "for all time to come" to "pure" Germans. The projected completion date was 1945, but instead of a new Olympic beginning, that year marked the end of the nightmare regime of Adolf Hitler and Nazi Germany.

5
THE OLYMPICS OF THE COLD WAR YEARS (1948-1960)

For eleven years, from 1937 through 1947, there were no Olympic Games. World War II not only caused the cancellation of the XII and XIII Olympiads, but it was the foundation for a different kind of war, known as the Cold War. The Cold War split the world into two political viewpoints: capitalist and Communist, led by the United States and the Soviet Union, respectively. This affected the Olympic Games, as they became more and more of a political as well as a sports arena. During the years between 1948 and 1960 politics influenced the Olympics as never before. But still there were many new Olympic heroes and heroines, admired by the world not so much for the country or political viewpoint they represented as for the athletic achievements they attained.

V WINTER OLYMPIAD, 1948

When peace finally returned to the world after the war, so did the Olympic Games. The Winter Olympics resumed in

1948 in St. Moritz, Switzerland. The games were preceded by stormy controversy that threatened to cancel the hockey championship. Two U.S. hockey teams were sent to the Olympics—one representing the U.S. Olympic Committee and the other sanctioned by the Amateur Hockey Association (AHA), which was recognized by the international hockey federation. The International Olympics Committee (IOC) ruled that neither American team could compete, then reversed itself and said the games could be played but that they would be non-Olympic events. Finally, it was ruled that the AHA team could compete but none of its games would count in the results. The twists and turns of the IOC rulings saved the hockey competition but created bad will for all concerned.

In 1948 the women's slalom was an Olympic event for the first time and was won by Gretchen Fraser of the United States. Dick Button, then an eighteen-year-old freshman at Harvard, won the men's skating championship and served notice about the powerhouse skaters being developed by the United States. Canada's Barbara Ann Scott was the outstanding woman skater.

XIV SUMMER OLYMPIAD, 1948

Unlike some of the Olympics prior to World War II, separate host countries were selected for the Winter and the Summer Games after the war. London was chosen as the setting for the 1948 Summer Games. There was some controversy about selecting a nation that had been deeply affected by the war and was suffering from a housing shortage, food rationing, and economic problems.

Despite the problems a record fifty-nine nations and 4,689 competitors took part in the XIV Games in London, and the English improvised wherever they could. At Wembley Stadium, for example, a temporary track was used for athletics. And various buildings were adapted for press, radio, and television coverage. School buildings and service camps became housing for athletes.

For the first time the premier athlete of the games was a woman, Fanny Blankers-Koen of the Netherlands. The thirty-year-old won four gold medals in track and field events—the 100-meter dash, the 200-meter dash, the 400-meter relay, and the 80-meter hurdles.

Other 1948 Olympic stars included seventeen-year-old Bob Mathias of the United States. Competing in only the third decathlon of his life, Mathias came from behind to triumph. The Czech Emil Zatopek set a new 10,000-meter mark.

One of the most inspirational stories of the 1948 Olympics involved the American Harrison Dillard. Winner of eighty-two straight hurdle races, he fell during the Olympic trials and failed to make the American team as a hurdler. Determined to be on the American team some way, Dillard entered the dash trial and made the U.S. squad. In London the great hurdler competed in the dash and the relay and won two gold medals. His was just another of the many inspirational stories that have become part of the history of the Olympics.

VI WINTER OLYMPIAD, 1952

Norway and Finland became the hosts for the 1952 Winter and Summer Olympics respectively—a first-time honor for each. The 1952 Winter Olympics began in Oslo, Norway, on both a controversial and inspirational note. The Russians had boycotted the Winter Olympics that year, and had refused to allow the Olympic torch access to Russian territory. This made the traditional torch trip from Greece impossible, because alternative routes would have been too long. Instead, the torch was lit from the house of Sondre Norheim, of Norway, the foremost pioneer of modern skiing. The Winter Games in Oslo were a success. Norway, considered

the homeland of skiing, was finally awarded the status of host to the Winter Games. A record thirty nations competed. Sondre Norheim's introduction of primitive heel bindings and a shaped ski revolutionized ski jumping and turning techniques. A record thirty nations competed in Norway. The Norwegians starred in the competitions, with Arnfinn Bergmann winning the ski jump, Stein Eriksen winning the giant slalom, and Hjalmar Anderson winning three speed skating events.

The American figure skater Dick Button won the men's single figure skating event, performing the first-ever triple rotation jump. Jeanette Altwegg of Great Britain won the women's figure skating competition but, surprisingly, decided not to become professional, and worked instead at managing the Pestalozzi Children's Village in Switzerland. When Germany won both the two-man and the four-man bobsled races, controversy ensued over the large size of the athletes. The International Bobsleigh Federation was forced to change its rules, limiting the weight of the teams to allow for fair competition.

XV SUMMER OLYMPIAD, 1952

A controversy far more complicated than the bobsled competition developed between 1948 and 1952 and dominated the Summer Olympics in Helsinki, Finland. The United States and the Soviet Union—allies during World War II—represented two different political viewpoints. At the time of the 1948 Olympics the two nations were already involved in the political conflict called the Cold War. In 1948,

Harrison Dillard (center) at the 1948 Olympics after tying the 100-meter dash record

however, the Russians chose not to compete in the Olympics. They announced that they would take part in the 1952 Games and preferred merely to observe the 1948 competition.

Soviet coaches and trainers came to London geared for "observing." Russian researchers took many photographs and accumulated thousands of pages of notes. They watched the athletic competition in foggy London and planned for the future.

Although the Russians did not compete in London, the Cold War climate was very much in evidence. When the games ended, several athletes from Hungary and Czechoslovakia refused to go back to their countries behind the Iron Curtain.

Between the games of 1948 and those of 1952 the Russians spent millions of dollars to develop international sports champions, using the facilities of their state-controlled program. For the Soviets, Olympic competition was seen as a test of strength between themselves and the United States.

The propaganda machines of the United States and Russia were very active in the months preceding the 1952 Olympics. The entire world awaited the first Olympic competition between the two superpowers.

The U.S. Olympic Committee staged an Olympic Telethon to raise money to counter what was called "The Red Menace." Singer Bing Crosby and comedian Bob Hope starred in the Telethon. "I guess Joe Stalin [the Russian leader] thinks he is going to show up our soft capitalistic Americans," joked Hope. "We're going to cut him down to size."

"There will be 71 nations in the Olympics at Helsinki," wrote Arthur Daley in the *New York Times*. "The United States would like to beat all of them, but the only one that counts is Soviet Russia. The Communist propaganda machine must be silenced so that there can't be even one distorted bleat out of it in regard to the Olympics. In

68

sports the Red brothers have reached the put-up-or-shut-up stage. Let's shut them up."

Avery Brundage, who was president of the IOC from 1952 to 1972, criticized the political controversy surrounding Olympic competition. "Sport . . . like music and the other fine arts, transcends politics," said Brundage. "We [of the Olympic movement] are concerned with sports, not politics and business."

The 1952 Helsinki Olympics were staged at a time when Russia and the United States were involved in military conflict in the Korean War. The Russians supported the North Koreans, while the United States was on the side of South Korea. This situation clouded Olympic competition.

The Helsinki Games—in fact, all athletic competition —was viewed by the Soviets as a test of their political system. "Each new victory is a victory for the Soviet form of society and the Socialist sport system," a Soviet spokesperson said. "It provides irrefutable proof of the superiority of socialist culture over the decaying culture of the capitalist states."

The Helsinki Games underscored the insulated way of life of the Soviets. All Russian athletes were kept away from those of the West. They lived in a separate "Eastern Camp" surrounded by barbed wire, along with athletes from the Russian satellites Hungary, Poland, Rumania, Czechoslovakia, and Bulgaria. No visitors were allowed into the Eastern Camp, where large pictures of the Russian ruler Joseph Stalin hung on the walls of the buildings.

While the participation of Russia in the Olympics was the big political story, other nations also had their share of the political controversy. East Germany was rejected by the IOC as a participant in the Olympics although West Germany was permitted to compete. Red China and Nationalist China (Taiwan) were both allowed to participate. However, Nationalist China boycotted the Olympics, and the Red Chinese contingent never showed up.

There were many outstanding performances by individuals and teams in the Helsinki Olympics, but the eyes of the world were on the unofficial competition between Russia and the United States. The Soviets finished with seventy-one medals, and the United States recorded seventy-six medals. Scoring was confused because of the lack of a formal system. In the Russian assessment they tied with the United States in the overall standings, 494–494. In the American scoring system the United States won, 614 to 553½. Regardless of the figures, the astonishing headline of the Helsinki Olympics was how well the Russians had done. American strength was evident in track and field, weight lifting, and swimming; the Russians were highly competitive in most other areas. That they would be a force to contend with in the future was evident.

A statement by Bob Mathias, Olympic decathlon champion, symbolized the mood of the American athletes in Helsinki: "There were many more pressures on the American athletes in 1952 than there were in 1948 because of the Russians. They were in a sense the real enemies. You just loved to beat 'em. You just had to beat 'em. It wasn't like beating some friendly country like Australia."

The Olympic conflicts of 1952 between the Russians and the Americans were a clash of political systems and also a clash of "professionals" versus "amateurs." Russian athletes were fully subsidized by the state, and in the American view they were professionals. The Soviets claimed that their athletes worked in the military, in civil service, and in the arts and that they were not paid for sports activity. The Russian system was "state amateurism." The United States insisted that whatever label the Russians applied to the way they handled their athletes it was a violation of the amateur code of the Olympics. Avery Brundage and the IOC refused to take a stand on the controversy. Brundage claimed that athletic scholarships to U.S. competitors could also be viewed as a violation of the Olympic spirit. There the matter rested, to be debated in the media and wherever sports fans and politicians gathered.

70

VII WINTER OLYMPIAD, 1956

In 1956 in Cortina, Italy, the Russians made their Winter Olympic appearance and won unofficial team honors, taking seven of a possible twenty-five gold medals and 121 points to 78½ for runner-up Austria. Toni Sailer, an Austrian skier, was the great individual star, becoming the second triple winner in Winter Olympic history by winning all three Alpine ski events. The American hockey team recorded its first victory ever over the Canadian hockey squad but was defeated in the championship game by the Soviet Union.

XVI SUMMER OLYMPIAD, 1956

Politics played an even more important role in the Summer Olympics than they did in the Winter Games. The Summer Games of 1956 scheduled for Melbourne, Australia, were preceded by two political crises that caused worldwide distress.

Backed by the Russians, Egypt tried to gain control of the Suez Canal, which had been a longtime free passage for oil to Western Europe. Israel, Great Britain, and France united to keep the Suez Canal open. Both the Soviet Union and the United States backed a United Nations cease-fire order. Egypt demanded that Israel, Great Britain, and France be barred from the Melbourne Games. The IOC rejected Egypt's demand, and Egypt, along with Lebanon and Iraq, boycotted the Olympics. The action by the three Arab nations—protest by boycott—moved the Olympics firmly into the political arena, setting a precedent for behavior that would be repeated again and again in the years ahead.

In Budapest, Hungarian workers and students took to the streets protesting Russian control of their nation. The Soviets sent troops and tanks to put a stop to what was called the Hungarian Revolution. Members of the Hungarian

Olympic team were en route to Melbourne when the fighting broke out. They considered returning home to fight the Russians rather than compete in Melbourne. However, with the Hungarian borders tightly secured by Russian troops, there was no way for them to return home.

What was taking place in Hungary triggered thoughts in several nations that the Olympics should be called off. Avery Brundage, head of the IOC, was insistent that the games go on. He said: "We are dead against any country using the Games for political purposes whether right or wrong . . . the Olympics belong to the people. They are contests for individuals and not of nations . . . every civilized person recoils in horror at the savage slaughter in Hungary, but that is no reason for destroying the nucleus of international cooperation."

Despite the Brundage arguments Spain, Switzerland, and the Netherlands withdrew from the Olympics because of the Russian invasion of Hungary. The Spanish Sport Federation explained that its athletes would not compete at games "while the liberties of people are being trampled on." The Dutch donated a large sum of money to Hungarian sufferers.

In another political controversy the nation of Taiwan withdrew from the Melbourne Olympics because Red China was admitted. And when the flag of Nationalist China (Taiwan) was accidentally raised over their camp, Red China withdrew from the Olympics.

Despite the political fireworks and military battles that preceded it, the Melbourne Games finally opened on November 22, 1956. Sixty-seven nations and approximately thirty-five hundred athletes—some Hungarian refugees who paid their own way—were on hand. Although a large sign on the stadium scoreboard proclaimed, "Classification by points on a national basis not recognized," all eyes were ready to count up the points in the battle for Olympic athletic supremacy between the Soviet Union and the United States.

Throughout the Olympics, Hungarians demonstrated

against and heckled the Russians. Hungarian athletes took down the flag over their quarters, tore off the Communist symbol, and sent up the flag of free Hungary.

A symbolic confrontation took place in the water polo semifinals between the Soviet Union and Hungary. In the stands Hungarians taunted the Russians. In the water the Hungarians took out their rage on the Soviet athletes. Hungary led 4 to 0 going into the final two minutes of the match. In a loose-ball struggle a Russian butted a Hungarian, drawing blood over that athlete's eye. Pandemonium prevailed among the pro-Hungarian crowd. The Russians exited the pool even though time still remained in the match.

"They were lucky to get out of the stadium alive," said Wally Wolf, a veteran water polo player from the United States.

When the final results of the Melbourne Olympics were tallied, the Russians had won thirty-seven gold medals, the United States thirty-two. The Soviet Union had recorded 722 points, and the United States had 593. Russia's improvement in all sports was the reason for its success.

The Melbourne Games, which had witnessed so much discord, ended on a note of harmony. During the final procession athletes did not march as part of their nations but instead ran, arms linked around each other, around the Olympic track. It was a testament to how individuals of all races, creeds, and political persuasions could ideally get along with each other. It was a symbol of the Olympic spirit: "The most important thing in the Olympic Games is not to win but to take part; the important thing in life is not the triumph but the struggle. The essential thing is not to have conquered but to have fought well."

VIII WINTER OLYMPIAD, 1960

Tension and controversy that had developed in the 1950s continued into the 1960s. The 1960 Winter Games were

scheduled for Squaw Valley, California, and again there were objections by European nations about a proposed Olympic site in the United States. The Europeans complained that the little town was too isolated and would not be able to provide adequate facilities for competition. These fears were not realized, as 9 million dollars was spent transforming the area into a remarkable sports complex. Attendance was second best in Olympic history to that point. One of the major upsets in Olympic history took place as the U.S. hockey team defeated both Canada and the Soviet Union and moved on to win the hockey gold. American skaters also dominated; David Jenkins and Carol Heiss both won gold medals.

An incident took place in the final game of the hockey competition that many thought symbolized good will between the superpowers. The United States, trailing a tough Czech team 4 to 3 after two periods, seemed out of breath. Nikola Sologubov, captain of the Russian hockey team, then used sign language to tell the Americans to inhale oxygen. Most of the U.S. players followed the Russian's advice. Back on the ice, the Americans went on to post a 9 to 4 triumph over the Czechs.

XVII SUMMER OLYMPIAD, 1960

Political controversy more serious than in the 1960 Winter Games preceded the Summer Olympics of 1960. In 1959

Politics superceded athletic competition during the 1956 Hungarian-Russian water polo match. Here, a Hungarian player is shown bleeding after a Russian competitor hit him. Despite this unsportsmanlike action, Hungary won the game 4–0.

75

Russia had raised the issue of the racial discrimination policies of South Africa. That nation's delegate to the IOC gave assurances of going along with the IOC policy of non-discrimination, and South Africa was allowed to participate in what some called "the games of good will." A record eighty-four nations and 5,902 athletes competed in the 1960 Summer Olympics.

The games were held in Rome, where the Italian Olympic Committee had spent 52 million dollars on new facilities that spread out all over the ancient city.

The U.S. track and field team came into the Olympics heavily favored. It never lived up to its promise, as it lost eight of the first eleven events it entered. Part of the American disappointment was symbolized by Boston's John Thomas, deemed the best high jumper. Thomas wound up third, behind two Russians.

There was further disappointment for Americans when for the first time since 1912 a country other than the United States won the 400-meter relay; the U.S. team was disqualified for an illegal pass of the baton.

Small nations, however, experienced Olympic success. The marathon was won by barefooted Abebe Bikila of Ethiopia. A Moroccan runner finished second. Pakistan defeated India to win the gold medal in field hockey. And two New Zealand runners won gold medals.

When the Olympic flame was extinguished in Rome, the final standings showed the Russian team with 103 medals to just 71 for the United States, its nearest rival. The

Although the U.S. track and field team as a whole did poorly at the 1960 Olympics, Wilma Rudolph won three gold medals. She was handicapped as a child and did not walk until she was eight years old.

Russian Olympic athletic superiority set off a furious debate in the United States, one that would set the tone for future Olympics.

Many in the United States read the Soviet Olympic triumph as a sign that America was weak. That triggered a strong emphasis on physical fitness in the administration of President John F. Kennedy, an attempt to bring the United States to the level of the Russians.

An American Legion spokesman argued: "We should stress victory, not merely participating. In the Olympics and international meets, only the winners are honored."

Hubert Humphrey, then a liberal Democratic senator from Minnesota, urged a financial effort by the American government to help win the Olympics. Humphrey spoke of "a relentless struggle between freedom and Communism [involving] almost every level of life from sprinters to spacemen." Humphrey attacked the Russians, arguing that they had turned the "once-idealistic Olympic Games into an ideological battlefield."

The assassination of President John F. Kennedy, however, as well as political problems, made the United States turn its attention to more demanding priorities, such as the Vietnam War. Humphrey's dream of federal funding of the Olympics was abandoned.

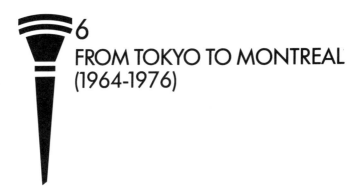

6
FROM TOKYO TO MONTREAL
(1964-1976)

Between 1964 and 1976, the Olympics remained full of political conflicts. However, the focus was less specifically on the competition between Russia and the United States and more on such rising controversies as South Africa's policy of apartheid, the increasing costs and complications of hosting an Olympics, the beginning and growth of commercialism in the games, the big business of televising the games, and the status of amateur athletes. By 1972, with all of this controversy and one terrible tragedy, the biggest question of all was being asked—whether or not the games should even continue.

IX WINTER OLYMPIAD, 1964

The Cold War attitude remained alive, although many other problems affected the outcome of the Winter Olympics of 1964. At Innsbruck, Austria, the site of the Winter Games, snow was in short supply, and three thousand Austrian soldiers had to haul snow from surrounding areas to pack the ski runs. Death and injury also marred the games. A Polish-born British luge rider was killed during a practice run, and an Austrian skier died after crashing into a tree. Three other athletes were also seriously injured. The Soviet Union maintained its Winter Olympic domination, leading all nations with eleven gold medals—seven of them accumulated by two Russian women schoolteachers. In 1961 the entire U.S. figure skating team had been killed in a plane crash en route to the world championships. At Innsbruck the badly handicapped American team was able to manage only one gold medal in skating—Terry McDermott won the gold in the 500-meter men's speed skating event.

XVIII SUMMER OLYMPIAD, 1964

Following the Winter Games, with their sporting triumphs and tragedies, political news occupied center stage at the Tokyo Olympics in the summer of 1964. As the games began, the globe was being circled by Russian cosmonauts. A nuclear device was exploded by the Communist Chinese government. Several Hungarians, dissatisfied with the quality of life under communism, defected to the West; and a pistol shooter from Nationalist China (Taiwan), for reasons he did not explain, went over to the East.

The Tokyo Olympics were in progress for only a few days when Nikita Khrushchev stepped down as the leader of the Soviet Union.

"I knew we were doing pretty well against the Russians," joked the head of the American Olympic Committee, "but I didn't know it would cause Khrushchev to resign."

South Africa's racial policies led to its being barred by the IOC from competing in the Tokyo Games. The ban on South Africa revealed the political power of emerging Third World sporting nations who felt they had something to prove at the Tokyo Olympics.

The United States came into the Tokyo Games with something to prove, too. At the Winter Olympics in Innsbruck, Austria, American athletes had suffered a disaster. Of thirty-four events, the Americans took first place in just one, compared with eleven for the Russians.

"It may be time," said a U.S. congressman, "to reconsider our traditional reluctance to provide governmental support to U.S. Olympic teams. The present situation is destructive for the athletes involved and destructive of team performance and morale."

The hidden meaning of these comments was that the United States was losing badly in the propaganda war with the Soviet Union as a result of the Russian stockpiling of Olympic gold medals.

The Japanese government spent 3 billion dollars to give Tokyo a facelift. The "Happy Games" was the theme of that XVIII Olympiad, which included a record 5,565 athletes representing a record 94 nations in a record 163 events. Stores and buildings were bright with Olympic decorations. A new high-speed railroad moved viewers to the Olympic Stadium.

The Tokyo Games served as a way for Japan to acquire badly needed urban renewal and new housing projects. However, it did much more than that. Just as the Winter Games of 1964 had been used by Austria to help promote the sales of ski equipment and polish the image of that nation as a tourist attraction, the Summer Games also served to give Japan an image as one of the world's great trading nations.

"Without the Olympics," said Tokyo Mayor Ryotaro Azuma, "Japan would not have risen to its high position in world trade so fast. Our national prestige depended on the Tokyo Games being a success."

The 1964 games were also a time of the first massive identification of athletic equipment and clothing with the Olympics. Firms realized the power and prestige of the games as a marketing vehicle. Until the 1964 games American athletes had never worn coordinated outfits. Now this changed, as athletes virtually modeled outfits provided at no charge by textile companies.

"Official" suppliers of other goods and services, television licensees, and others became more and more a source of money for the International Olympic Committee (IOC) and the nations involved in the games.

Subsidies—money given to athletes and the Olympic movement—became more and more widespread with the 1964 Olympics and have continued unabated to this day. Traditionally, the Soviet Union and various Third World nations totally financed their Olympic athletes. Athletic scholarships and other favors had begun to be extended to athletes in the United States. Other Olympic performers identified with manufacturers benefited through cash payments.

Avery Brundage, speaking as the head of the IOC, called the games "a revolt against twentieth century materialism . . . [as] a devotion to a cause and not the reward." Unfortunately, although the games brought out the best in the human spirit, concern for financial rewards became as important to many in the Olympics as devotion to a cause.

One of the most positive things about the Tokyo Olympics that made them the "Happy Games" was that newspapermen went along with IOC urgings that unofficial team point standings be dropped. Newspapers reported only the total medals won, nation by nation.

The final statistics for the 1964 Olympics showed the Soviet Union with ninety-six gold medals to ninety for the United States. Russia also had a slight edge in the unofficial point totals. Nevertheless, American pride was eased by its team's remarkable comeback from the disappointments at Rome.

Ethiopian pride swelled at the exploits of marathon runner Abebe Bikila. The small, slim athlete had stunned the world by winning his event in the Rome Olympics. His time there was three minutes better than his previous

Olympic best. Just five weeks before the scheduled running of the Tokyo Olympics marathon, Bikila was operated on for appendicitis. Experts gave him no chance even to run the marathon in 1964, much less win it. Bikila not only won, he set a new Olympic time, finishing minutes ahead of his nearest rival.

Other memorable accomplishments at the Tokyo Games included Australia's Dawn Fraser's third straight Olympic triumph in the 100-meter swim race, America's Al Oerter's third consecutive Olympic discus win, and America's Joe Frazier's victory in heavyweight boxing.

At the closing ceremony, national conflicts and increasing commercialism notwithstanding, the spirit of the Olympics still prevailed. Hundreds of Japanese schoolchildren encircled the darkened stadium floor. On signal each lit a torch, and the illuminated scoreboard flashed out the word *Sayonara*.

X WINTER OLYMPIAD, 1968

By 1968 the Olympics had become big business and a big television hit. Not only were more and more athletes and nations participating in each Olympiad, but more spectators than ever before were able to see the Olympics, thanks to television. Some athletes with remarkable performances became sports heroes overnight, while others used the games as a platform to express their opinions. And television captured all of the action.

American television paid 3 million dollars for the rights to telecast the 1968 Winter Olympics in Grenoble, France. It was television coverage that made Frenchman Jean-Claude Killy a media celebrity, focusing on the handsome athlete's Alpine triple victories in the downhill, slalom, and giant slalom. Unfortunately, the U.S. Winter Olympic team once again fell below expectations. Only one gold medal was recorded by the Americans; it was awarded to Peggy

Fleming for figure skating. The Soviets also slipped in their overall performance, as smaller countries like Norway, Sweden, and the Netherlands gained strength.

XIX SUMMER OLYMPIAD, 1968

The American team fared much better in the Summer Games held in Mexico City. However, controversy afflicted the games in many ways before they began and during the competition.

Numerous nations objected to the selection of Mexico City as an Olympic site because it was more than 7,000 feet above sea level. It was pointed out that competition there would provide an unfair advantage to athletes accustomed to a high altitude and would handicap others not used to thin air.

To cut down objections the IOC ruled that athletes could train in high altitudes for four weeks in the last three months before the Mexico City Olympics to accustom themselves to that environment. The IOC action pleased some lowland nations, but at the same time it was a real softening of the classic amateur rule to allow this advantage.

An even more serious controversy arose over the issue of South Africa. That nation's policy of apartheid, racial discrimination, made it an outlaw in the eyes of many countries, especially those of black Africa. The IOC had allowed South Africa to compete in the 1960 Games in Rome after receiving assurances from their IOC delegate that South Africa would comply with Olympic principles of nondiscrimination. Soon it became apparent that despite the position of the South African National Olympic Committee, the South African government had no intention of permitting fully integrated sports. Therefore, the IOC banned South Africa from the Tokyo Olympics of 1964.

In January 1968 a three-member IOC commission reported that South Africa had made reforms. IOC president Avery Brundage was pleased, and he argued that the real issue was not South Africa's apartheid policies but racism in Olympic sports. IOC members then voted to readmit South Africa to the Olympic Games in Mexico City.

That news triggered protests among almost all of the African nations and some other Third World countries, which threatened to withdraw from the games if South Africa competed. The Soviet Union also threatened a boycott. Many black athletes from the United States indicated that they, too, planned to boycott the games.

As a face-saving device for both the IOC and South Africa, the IOC announced that the climate of "violence" in the world made it necessary to bar South Africa from the games in Mexico City. Two years later South Africa would be expelled from the Olympic movement.

A third major problem of the XIX Olympiad was that various groups in Mexico were unhappy that their country had been selected as an Olympic site. They claimed that the money the government of Mexico would spend could be better spent on things that would help the people and improve the quality of life in their nation.

University students staged demonstrations against the government, calling for educational and police reforms. Three weeks before the games were to begin, tanks were stationed outside Mexico City University opposite the main Olympic stadium. The atmosphere was tense.

On October 2, 1968—ten days before the games were scheduled to take place—thousands demonstrated in the Square of the Three Cultures in Mexico City. The military surrounded the square. More than 260 people were killed and 1,200 were injured in the five-hour battle that followed. The bloodbath ended all protests against the government.

On October 12, 1968, the games began under the curious slogan "Everything is possible with peace." Enriqueta Basilo, the first woman to light the Olympic flame, opened the 1968 games.

The games went on despite the problems. Nearly eight

thousand athletes from 112 nations competed in a fiesta-like atmosphere in Mexico City, and the 1968 games went on to rank as one of the most successful Olympics in history.

One of the most controversial moments occurred when U.S. black athletes Tommie Smith, gold medal winner in the 200-meter run, and John Carlos, winner of the bronze medal in the same event, stood on the podium to receive their medals.

Using the moment to make a political statement, the two athletes bowed their heads while the U.S. national anthem was played and then raised black-gloved fists in a "Black Power" salute. Their actions set off a storm of debate all over the world. Both men were suspended from the games and expelled from the Olympic Village.

Carlos explained later that he wanted to show that blacks "were not some kind of work horse" who "can perform and they can throw us some peanuts and say good boy, good boy." Carlos continued: "When Tommie and I got on the stand, we knew we weren't alone. We knew that everyone that was watching at home was upon the stand with us. We wanted to let the world know about the problems of black people, and we did our thing and stepped down. We believe we were right. We'd do it again tomorrow."

The United States won seven gold medals in eleven boxing events in the Mexico City Olympics. The heavyweight division winner was George Foreman, a nineteen-year-old black. He waved an American flag as he walked around the ring after his final bout. Foreman claimed he

Tommie Smith (center) and John Carlos (right) giving the controversial Black Power salute during the awards ceremony

86

wasn't making any kind of "demonstration," that he was "just proud to be an American."

The American basketball team won the gold medal, led by two black stars, Spencer Haywood and Jo Jo White. Lew Alcindor, now better known as Kareem Abdul-Jabbar, was at that time the star of UCLA's championship basketball team. He had passed up the Olympics in sympathy with the announced black boycott that never took place.

Many believed that the high altitude enabled Africans to make an astonishing sweep of distance running: Kenya's Kip Keino, 1,500 meters; Tunisia's Mohammed Gammoudi, 5,000 meters; Kenya's Naftali Temu, 10,000 meters; Kenya's Amos Biwott, 3000-meter steeplechase; and Ethiopia's Mamo Wolde, marathon.

The games of the XIX Olympiad also produced the first victim of drug testing—an issue that would haunt all future games. A Swedish pentathlon medalist was disqualified after being accused of using an illegal substance, alcohol.

The Olympics ended much more happily than they had begun. The closing ceremonies captured everyone's attention with their festiveness and energy. Mexico City would long be remembered for this special celebration.

XI WINTER OLYMPIAD, 1972

The year 1972 was filled with dilemmas. Triumph and tragedy, along with a great deal of tension, combined to rule over the games more powerfully and significantly than ever before. The Winter Olympics of 1972 in Sapporo, Japan, were marred by acrimony. Avery Brundage, the eighty-four-year-old president of the IOC, almost brought a halt to the games by threatening to disqualify a number of European skiers for alleged violations of the amateur code. Brundage also sought to change the Alpine events into world championships rather than keeping them under the

Olympic banner, which would have cost the Olympic movement a few million dollars in lost television revenue. Ultimately, Austria's Karl Schranz became Brundage's scapegoat and was barred from competing. Schranz was an open critic of the Olympic ideal, and there were reports that he had made as much as fifty thousand dollars a year as a skier. Other athletes threatened to quit the Winter Games because of the expulsion of Schranz, but they were persuaded to remain and the games went on.

XX SUMMER OLYMPIAD, 1972

The 1972 Summer Olympics staged in Munich, Germany, showcased great athletic talent, but it also underscored international tensions, disagreements, bias, and terror.

Even before the games got underway there was controversy. Several African nations threatened to boycott the Olympics if Rhodesia, ruled by whites, was allowed to compete. Rhodesia was barred from the games.

That tension was minor compared to the terror that took place one hour before dawn on September 5, 1972. Eight Arab terrorists climbed over the fence surrounding the Olympic Village and burst into the quarters of the Israeli team. Two Israelis were murdered and nine survivors were taken hostage.

The world was shocked and saddened by the news. Throughout the day crowds gathered outside the Olympic Village protesting the continuation of the games. For the next fifteen hours demands were made and bargaining went on between the terrorists, members of the fanatical Black September group, and authorities. The terrorists demanded the release of two hundred Arab guerrillas in Israel and elsewhere in return for sparing the lives of the Israeli captives. Television cameras showed the world the compound where the tense drama was being played out. The image of an armed terrorist, stocking mask over his head,

symbolized how the Olympic Games had become a pawn of international politics.

An agreement was finally reached that was to have granted the terrorists safe passage to an Arab nation. A helicopter took captors and captives out of the Olympic compound and to an airfield. There German sharpshooters fired at the terrorists. In the gunfight that followed, the nine Israeli hostages were killed; three of the terrorists died, and three others were captured. The irony of the whole sad and frightening experience was that the German government had hoped to have the Munich Olympics lessen the memories of Nazism and the terrible treatment of Jews during World War II. Now Jewish blood was once again shed on German soil; but this time, in an ironic twist, Germans were attempting to rescue Jews.

Through all the hysteria and tragedy the games were allowed to continue.

"I am sure the public will agree," Avery Brundage said, "that we cannot allow a handful of terrorists to destroy the nucleus of international cooperation and good will we have in the Olympic movement. The Games must go on and we must continue our efforts to keep them clean, pure and honest, and try to extend the sportsmanship of the athletic field into other areas."

The IOC argued that "an end to the Games would mean a victory for terrorism." Instead of canceling the Olympics, the IOC staged a memorial ceremony in honor of the eleven Israeli athletes who died.

Red Smith, the noted sportswriter of the *New York Times*, called Brundage "the high priest of the playground"

On September 5, 1972, this image of terrorism is what the world saw instead of Olympic competition.

and went on to sharply attack the officials of the IOC. "Walled off in their dream world," Smith wrote, "appallingly unaware of the realities of life and death, the aging playground directors who conduct the quadrennial music dance ruled that a little blood must not be allowed to interrupt play."

There was also controversy on the basketball court. The U.S. basketball team entered the Olympics with a sixty-three-game winning streak that dated back to 1936.

The championship game at Munich pitted the American team against the team from the Soviet Union. Surprisingly, the Russians led 49 to 48 with three seconds left to play in the game. Doug Collins, who would go on to be a professional player in the National Basketball Association, was fouled by two charging Soviet players. Collins lost consciousness. When he revived, he made two foul shots, and the Americans started to celebrate, thinking time had now run out and they had won the game, 50 to 49.

An official claimed that the Soviets had called a time out and that one second still remained in the game. The Russians threw the ball the length of the court but failed to score as time ran out. However, the head official brought up some obscure technicality and added three more seconds of playing time.

The Americans were infuriated. It seemed as if the Russians would keep shooting until they won. A full court pass went to the seven-foot Russian center, Alexsandr Belov. He jammed the ball into the basket, and the Soviet Union managed a controversial 51-to-50 victory over the United States.

The officiating was definitely biased in the eyes of

Grieving Israeli athletes
during the memorial service held
in honor of their teammates

93

most observers; however, the U.S. team lost its appeal. In protest the American basketball players refused to accept their silver medals.

A bicycle road race also became a platform for political statement and controversy. Seven members of the Irish Republican Army (I.R.A.) managed to make their way into the crowded start of the race. One of them caused an entanglement of bicycles that resulted in a fifteen-bike accident.

Electronic timing was kept for precise judgments in races and events that came down to split seconds. However, subjective judging in various events such as boxing, gymnastics, and diving seemed to bring out nationalistic biases on the part of the judges. And this caused major disputes and controversies.

U.S. boxer Reginald Jones, for example, virtually pounded Soviet fighter Valery Tregubov into a bloody pulp; however, the judges announced that the Soviet contestant was the winner of the match. Some other American boxers, divers, and gymnasts suffered from the same biased treatment at the hands of Iron Curtain judges.

An East German won the pole vault competition when performers like Bob Seagren of the United States and Kjell Isaksson of Sweden were not allowed to use fiberglass poles.

A gold medal was stripped from America's Rick DeMont. He had won the 400-meter freestyle, but it was pointed out that he had taken a drug for his asthmatic condition before the competition. Although the drug was used to treat asthma, it was also on the list of illegal substances for Olympic athletes.

A scene of confusion between coaches, referees, and officials at the conclusion of the controversial U.S.-Soviet Union basbetball game

Despite the terrible tragedy of the murdered Israelis and the raging controversies in the sport competitions, some incredible athletes shone in their events and brought pride to their countries and their sports. Mark Spitz of the United States won a record seven gold medals in swimming, winning and setting world records in each event he entered. Olga Korbut, who until the Munich Olympics was an unknown Russian gymnast, not only won two individual gold medals in gymnastic competition but captured the hearts of millions around the world and brought an unprecedented popularity to her sport.

The Munich Olympics—a mixture of tragedy, controversy, and marvelous athletic accomplishment—finally came to an end. One billion television viewers around the globe had watched it. And the world wondered about the validity of Avery Brundage's comment about the games: "We have only the strength of a great ideal and it cannot be stopped by anyone."

XII WINTER OLYMPIAD, 1976

Although emotions ran high as the very existence of the Olympic Games was debated in 1972 and afterward, the games did continue in 1976. While not nearly as marred by controversy as the 1972 Games, the 1976 Olympics had their share of problems.

The location of a site for the 1976 Winter Olympics once again led to debate and dispute. Denver, Colorado, had originally been selected as the site to coincide with the two-hundredth anniversary of the American Revolution. However, environmentalists in Colorado felt that holding the Olympics in Denver was a threat to the ecology. They maintained that it would encourage real estate developers and lead to damage to the environment. Cost estimates for the building of a Denver Olympic site also continued to skyrocket, and in November 1972 Colorado voters, in large numbers, approved a referendum to bar further expenditures of public money for a Winter Olympics site in Denver.

Innsbruck, Austria, became the actual site of the 1976 Winter Olympics. Thirty-seven nations and 1,128 athletes were represented, but long-time IOC president Avery Brundage was missing for the first time in a quarter century. Having resigned his post after the Munich Olympics, he died at the age of eighty-seven in May 1975.

American athletes provided the surprises of the Innsbruck Games, to the delight of the huge American television audience. The speed skaters, led by Sheila Young, won six medals in eight events; Dorothy Hamill returned the women's figure skating championship to the United States, showing off a flawless style, beauty, and a stylish hairdo. Others who captured the fancy of fans included the tiny nation of Liechtenstein, with a population of twenty-three thousand, whose athletes won two gold medals; West Germany's Rosi Mittermaier, star of women's Alpine skiing, who almost won all three events; and the Russian pairs skaters, Irina Rodnina and Aleksandr Zaitsev, whose ability and incredible skating combinations were so greatly admired.

A drug incident occurred in the ice hockey competition. The Czech team had contracted a very bad case of the flu that swept the Olympic Village. Because one of the Czech players took flu medication that contained a banned drug, the Czech victory against Poland was taken away from them. They went on to lose the final game to Russia by a narrow margin.

Perhaps the single event best remembered by the crowd at Innsbruck as well as the television viewers was the downhill race. Austrian Franz Klammer captured the hearts of his countrymen, as no other athlete had, in an incredible downhill race. Anyone who saw it was left breathless by his amazing agility and speed as he raced down the slopes to come from behind and win the gold medal.

XXI SUMMER OLYMPIAD, 1976

Even before the start of the 1976 Summer Olympic Games in Montreal, Canada, there were problems. The rate of progress and the quality of construction of facilities for the games did not please members of the IOC. There was concern that the facilities would not be completed in time for the games, and there were suggestions to move the 1976 Olympics to another site.

Montreal had budgeted 310 million dollars for the games, a sum that proved to be far too small to cover the escalating costs of hosting an Olympics. The provincial government of Quebec pitched in with financial assistance to Montreal to help pay the final Olympic bill, which was estimated at 1.5 billion dollars. The staggering cost of hosting the games was debated, as well as the question of whether the benefits of serving as an Olympic host were worth the financial costs.

Another controversial issue at Montreal involved New Zealand. That nation had sent a rugby team to compete in South Africa in the early summer of 1976. African nations demanded that the IOC expel New Zealand from the Montreal Games for competing against a nation that practiced apartheid. The IOC refused to ban New Zealand from the games, arguing that rugby was not an Olympic sport and pointing out that New Zealand did not practice apartheid.

Just forty-eight hours before the games were scheduled to begin, two dozen African countries and their supporters pulled out of the Montreal Olympics, reducing the competitive field by about 450 athletes. Although some African athletes paid their own way to the games, hoping to compete under the Olympic flag, IOC officials refused to allow them to participate.

An additional controversy at the Montreal Games involved Taiwan. Canada had officially recognized the People's Republic of China (Communist China). Almost on the eve of the Olympics the government of Canada announced that it would not allow participation by Taiwan athletes under the flag and name of the Republic of China.

A huge storm of protest developed over this issue. Threats to cancel the games were put forward by the IOC. The United States indicated that it would withdraw from the games if Taiwan was excluded. Canada remained steadfast on the issue. Finally, Taiwan withdrew from the games on its own, but U.S. Secretary of State Henry Kissinger spurned an invitation to attend the games because of Canada's position.

Tight, heightened security was everywhere—the result of the tragedy at Munich. There were those who wanted some type of memorial staged at Montreal for the slain Israeli athletes, but the IOC rejected the idea. On the other hand, the IOC honored the memory of eleven workers who lost their lives in construction accidents at the Montreal facilities. The families of those construction workers were given free tickets to Olympic events.

All types of surprises and incidents characterized the Montreal Olympics. The Soviet Union managed to obtain only two gold medals in men's track and field, while the small nations of Jamaica, Cuba, and Trinidad swept the men's 100-, 200-, and 800-meter events.

Margaret Murdoch, a thirty-three-year-old nursing student from Kansas, tied in shooting with teammate Lanny Bassham. Judges voted to give Bassham the win on the basis of better placement of final-round shots. Then, in a grand gesture, Bassham insisted that Murdoch also have a place on the victory stand.

Boris Onischenko, Soviet pentathlete, was charged with electronic cheating when he tampered with the wiring of his epée in the fencing section of his event. He was sent home to the Soviet Union in disgrace.

Russia was the flashpoint of a number of minor incidents created by the Ukranian émigré population that lives north of Montreal. Various demonstrations were staged by the Ukranians against the Soviet Union, including the burning of a Soviet flag outside the Olympic Village.

East Germany recorded forty gold medals and a total of ninety-four medals at the Montreal Games. It was an astonishing accomplishment for a nation with a population of only 17 million people.

A superbly efficient system produces East German athletes who are scouted, screened, and tested at an early age. Kornelia Ender personified this system. At Montreal she won four gold medals to lead East German women swimmers to victory in eleven of their thirteen events. The criticisms of the "state" method of developing athletes is that they are skilled and they win, but they do not seem to be having any fun. The East German reply was "It isn't possible to do this well [excel in the Olympics] and not have fun."

The state system used by East Germany and Russia— training athletes, subsidizing them, and taking care of all of their needs—was attacked by critics as a way of thinly disguising what were in fact professional athletes. And this has developed into still another continuing controversy that affects the entire Olympic movement.

With all of its problems the Montreal Olympics still served as a showcase for most of the great amateur athletes in the world. And in the closing ceremonies there were some memorable moments. Five hundred women dressed in white formed five interlocking rings. Then they

Here, the state system is in evidence as East German children between the ages of four and six are given swimming lessons at a government-supported gym called a sports halle.

removed their robes, revealing the bright colors of the circle symbols. Indian tribes of Canada marched in splendid and colorful native costumes. And finally, the Indians, the athletes, and the spectators danced on the field of Olympique Stadium until the early hours of the morning.

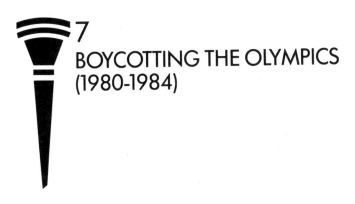

7
BOYCOTTING THE OLYMPICS
(1980-1984)

Before the 1980s boycotting the Olympics was acted out on a rather limited basis. Most of the time countries did not participate because they were barred, not because they chose to stay away.

Suddenly, in the 1980s the two most influential nations of the world—the United States and the Soviet Union—each boycotted a Summer Olympics. Other nations followed their lead. By boycotting the games these two countries changed the perception of the Olympic Games dramatically. Was their purpose to have nations of the world join together in sports competition, or was it more important that the Olympics be used by nations as a political arena?

XIII WINTER OLYMPIAD, 1980

The ongoing ideological battle between the United States and the Soviet Union has become a continuing sports confrontation in the Olympics: communism versus democracy

103

—one political system against another. In general, Soviet athletes, trained in a state system of what many call "thinly disguised professionalism" have come out on top in overall Olympic competition in recent years.

That is why what happened in the ice hockey competition in the 1980 Winter Games at Lake Placid stands out as a symbolic example of the style and substance of the two nations in the Olympics.

Neither Russia nor the United States boycotted the Winter Olympics of 1980 and 1984; only the Summer Olympics were so strongly affected. In four straight Winter Olympics before 1980 the Big Red (Russian) hockey machine had won gold medals. Their team did not lose a single game in 1972 or 1976. The Russians boasted a combination of speed skating, team discipline, and precision passing. In exhibition games against top performers of the professional National Hockey League the Russians made virtually every contest close.

In an exhibition game shortly before the Olympics in Lake Placid the Soviets demolished the young United States Olympic team by 10 to 3.

"You defense them one way," grumbled Herb Brooks, the American coach, "they come at you another way. You know what our chances are in the Olympics against them— slim to none."

The players on the U.S. hockey team were not the best collegiate performers in the United States, but Brooks had selected them with "coachability" in mind. He wanted players who would be disciplined and who would work as a team.

A long exhibition season in Europe and the United States shaped the American hockey team. They learned to play as a team, relying on passing and unselfishness to set up teammates for a shot, to set offensive plays, and to control the puck. They learned how to play to win and not to beat themselves.

The Americans tied Sweden, 2 to 2, in the opening

round of the Olympic hockey tournament but didn't look too effective doing it. However, the team came to life against Czechoslovakia, the defending European champion. Behind goalie Jim Craig, captain Mike Eruzione, and forward Mark Johnson, the Americans overpowered the Czechs, 7 to 3. Then they romped to a 5-to-1 triumph over Norway.

"Who knows?" smiled Eruzione. "We may be doing something nobody dreamed of us doing."

On a Friday night that many Americans still remember the youthful U.S. hockey team was matched against the squad from the Soviet Union, a group of pros considered one of the best teams in the world.

It was a difficult time in the United States. There had been attacks on American embassies; there was the Iranian hostage crisis; there was the Soviet invasion of Afghanistan. U.S. prestige in the world was at a low ebb.

In bars, hotel rooms, living rooms, and on college campuses millions watched the ice hockey confrontation between the Soviet Union and the United States.

The Russians scored two first-period goals. It seemed that the inevitable Russian victory was just a matter of time. However, by the end of the first period the American team had tied the score. Incredibly, with just six minutes left to go in the contest, the U.S. team went ahead for good. The final score was 4 to 3.

"U.S.A., U.S.A." That chant echoed at Lake Placid and throughout America. In that war on ice between East and West, in that competition between the Soviet Union and the United States, the Americans had come out on top. It showed how teamwork, drive, and dedication can pay off. It symbolized the victory of the amateur over the professional and, to some, the triumph of one system of government over another. The "Miracle at Lake Placid" was one hockey game, but its symbolic meaning was not lost on the world.

The gold medal match was against Finland. The U.S. team was down by a goal heading into the final period. But

An exuberant American hockey team and their fans celebrate the surprise victory over the Russians.

the Americans rallied to score three goals and defeat Finland, 4 to 2, and win the gold. It was an exciting moment in Olympic history.

Another performance at the 1980 Winter Olympics that cheered Americans and thrilled sports fans all over the world was that of American speed skater Eric Heiden. He won five individual medals in an astounding show of endurance, power, and speed.

Although the Winter Games were dominated in the medal standings by the East Germans and the Russians, memorable performances by the U.S. hockey team, by Eric Heiden, and by other Americans provided inspirational stories for a nation in need of new heroes.

XXII SUMMER OLYMPIAD, 1980

The rivalry and antagonisms between the United States and the Soviet Union were clearly demonstrated in the way Moscow was chosen to be the host for the 1980 Games. Both Los Angeles and Moscow had submitted bids for the 1976 Summer Games. Surprisingly, however, on the second ballot Montreal was selected as the site.

The Soviets were angered and charged that the two North American cities had conspired to deprive Moscow of the games. Los Angeles Mayor Sam Yorty noted that although his city did not get the games, he was at least happy that the Olympics would remain in the "free world."

When the matter of the site for the 1980 games came up, only Los Angeles and Moscow submitted bids. Many nations objected to the Russian city as a location for the Olympics. Israel lodged a protest, pointing to examples of "racism and anti-Semitism" at the World University Games held in Moscow in 1973. More than forty U.S. congressmen, plus the U.S. Olympic Committee, went on record as opposed to Moscow as a site for the 1980 Olympics.

Nevertheless, the International Olympic Committee

(IOC), impressed by Russian assurances of fair play and wishing to stage the Olympics for the first time in a Communist nation, selected Moscow as the site for the 1980 Summer Olympics. In general, Americans went along with the decision. It was felt that a new detente (a period of getting along between the two superpowers) would be served by having Moscow as an Olympic site.

In 1979 Soviet troops invaded Afghanistan. Any harmony or detente between the Soviet Union and the United States was now impossible. President Jimmy Carter was outraged and announced in early January 1980 that America would not take part in the Moscow Olympics if the Russians did not withdraw their troops.

The Soviets claimed they had been invited into Afghanistan to clear up internal problems and would not leave until that was accomplished. President Carter prevailed with his total boycott plan, which resulted in no American athletes competing, very few American spectators attending, and limited U.S. television coverage. All of this resulted in loss of revenue for the Olympics.

The United States put much pressure on other countries to boycott the games also, creating tension between national Olympic committees and their governments. The Conservative government of Great Britain elected to support President Carter; however, the British Olympic Committee voted to participate in the Moscow Games.

The Australian Olympic Committee voted 6 to 5 to send a team to Moscow but also allowed each sports federation to make its own decision. Four of the federations decided not to go to Moscow.

When the games opened, sixty-two nations, including the United States, Japan, West Germany, and Canada, were among those missing. There were fewer than six thousand athletes competing. The 1980 games were referred to as "the Eastern European Olympics."

The Russians staged a grand opening ceremony. Soviet men and women, garbed in the tunics of ancient Greece, sprinkled rose petals on the track before the teams of athletes came onto the field. Five thousand card-holders flashed brilliantly colored pictures as five thousand pigeons flew above Lenin Stadium.

Despite the splendor of the Soviet show, the sadness of the XXII Olympiad and all the missing nations and athletes was underscored in the opening ceremony. Sixteen of the eighty-one teams that competed in Moscow refused to carry their national flags in the march in the opening ceremony. A solitary British flag-bearer moved stiffly and carried the five-ringed Olympic flag instead of the Union Jack. Five athletes from New Zealand marched behind a black flag on which was superimposed a white olive branch of peace and the five interlocking rings of the Olympic emblem.

The Soviet Union and the German Democratic Republic (East Germany) won the bulk of the medals. Of the 205 gold medals awarded, the Soviet Union recorded 80 and East Germany won 47. Warsaw Pact countries— those allied with Russia—were the four top medal-winning nations. The Soviet Union won a total of 195 medals, and East Germany won 126. There could have been a complete runaway by the two Communist nations if not for the strong showing by Great Britain and Ethiopia in track and field.

Throughout the Moscow Games there were silent protests and lots of discussion about the state of the Olympics. Critics suggested that the 1980 boycott revealed that the games should be staged in a neutral site to take them out of the realm of politics. Others objected to national anthems being played and flags of nations raised, claiming that these nationalistic symbols only increased the political nature of the games.

When the Moscow Olympics came to an end, fifty-six new Olympic records and thirty-nine world records had been set. There were a host of new winning heroes. Allan Wells of England became the first Briton to outsprint the world in the 100 meters since Harold Abrahams in 1924;

England's Daley Thompson won the decathlon; Steve Ovett and Sebastian Coe triumphed in the 800- and 1,500-meter races, respectively; Cuba's Teofilo Stevenson clinched his third straight heavyweight victory; and Ethiopia's Miruts Yifter, a third-place finisher in Munich who was deprived of participation in Montreal because of the African boycott, outkicked his much younger opponents and triumphed in the 5,000 and 10,000 meters.

The losers were all of the athletes of the world who did not compete—cut off from their chance by the politics of nations and the whims of politicians. American athletes were presented with Congressional Olympic medals at the White House, but this was small consolation for many who had trained for years to compete in the 1980 Olympics in Moscow.

XIV WINTER OLYMPIAD, 1984

The United States and other nations that had boycotted the 1984 Summer Games returned to the 1984 Winter Olympics. These Winter Games took place at Sarajevo, Yugoslavia, in February 1984, bringing together 1,510 competitors representing forty-nine nations. It was a brilliant episode for the "White Games," which had begun as an afterthought to the Summer Games and were now firmly established as an integral part of the Olympic movement.

East Germany, the Soviet Union, and the United States dominated the competition. Debbie Armstrong won the first U.S. victory in the women's giant slalom, with her teammate Christin Cooper taking second place. Michela Figini of Switzerland won the women's downhill, and Paoletta Magoni of Italy took the women's slalom.

American Bill Johnson was a major surprise, finishing first in the Olympic downhill skiing event, the first American man to win the gold medal in Alpine skiing. He had predicted he would win before the competition even started. Some people were offended by his brashness, while others admired his self-confidence. Scott Hamilton charmed the crowds and television viewers, winning the men's singles in figure skating. British ice dancers Jayne Torvill and Christopher Dean became skating stars, receiving twelve perfect scores of six and a great deal of publicity and acclaim for their artistic performances.

Organizers of the games staged them without one major flaw. The only disappointment was the heavy snow that forced frequent rescheduling of the skiing events. The postponements were very expensive for ABC-TV, as was the disappointing performance of the U.S. hockey team.

The other major problem for television was that all of the shows were taped, and the six-hour time difference between Sarajevo and the eastern United States meant that potential viewers already knew the results before the programs were shown. Television audiences were 25 percent below expectations, and ABC had to reimburse many of the Olympic sponsors for the losses.

Overall, however, the Winter Games in Sarajevo were a great success filled with great athletic talent.

XXIII SUMMER OLYMPIAD, 1984

After the first Los Angeles Olympics were staged in 1932, the Southern California Committee for the Olympic Games was formed. Its aim was to have the Olympics return to Los Angeles. It took forty years, but the City of Angels was rewarded with a return engagement.

Los Angeles taxpayers were well aware of the huge debts accumulated by the city of Montreal and refused to assume financial responsibility for the games. The IOC was alarmed at suggestions that a private corporation would be responsible for the games, for in the past host governments had always assumed the costs. The IOC provisionally awarded the games to Los Angeles, and then months of tough negotiations followed.

Finally, a distinctly American solution to the controversy was arrived at. The costs of the games would in fact be borne by a private corporation. It was a revolutionary agreement—Olympic Games run by a private committee with no ties to the government, operating on funds raised in the private sector.

The Los Angeles Olympic Organizing Committee announced its plans for a "Spartan Olympics." Its president, Peter V. Ueberroth, pledged to minimize costs and retain high Olympic standards. The committee's very low operating budget was estimated at 500 million dollars, to be raised from sponsorships, ticket sales, and television rights.

The lessons of Montreal were on everyone's mind, and further controversy arose over the private corporation's Spartan Olympics theme. Some critics claimed that the high standards of the Olympics would not be met with all of the planned cutting of costs.

One factor that greatly aided the Los Angeles Olympic Organizing Committee was the funds generated from television rights. ABC-TV paid a record 225 million dollars for the U.S. rights. The network assembled 2,500 technicians, 56 cameras, 660 miles of cable, and 2 communications satellites. And American viewers were given nearly two hundred hours of Olympic programming—almost 2½ times as much programming as had been allotted to the Montreal Olympics.

A major criticism that preceded the Los Angeles Games was that they were spread out as never before—almost 4,500 miles connected by 414 miles of freeway. This resulted in events being scheduled in widely separated venues. For example, a British rower at Lake Casitas and a French equestrian rider at Fairbanks Ranch 195 miles to the south would have been closer to each other had they stayed at home in Southampton and Paris. Nevertheless, despite these logistical problems and the criticisms of those anxious to put down the Los Angeles Games, the scattered nature of the sites did not prove to be a problem.

Neither did the dire predictions about massive traffic jams on the Los Angeles freeways, the smog, the sweltering summer heat, the high prices, and the crowded hotels.

Coping and coping well became the order of the day, thanks to the efficiency of the organizers and an army of volunteer workers.

One thing that the Los Angeles Olympic Organizing Committee could not control was the action of the Soviet Union and some of its supporters. Shortly before the games began they announced a boycott. The Russians claimed that they were concerned about the security of their athletes in Los Angeles. The hidden motive was to reciprocate for the U.S. boycott of the 1980 Olympics in Moscow.

Once again the games became a sounding board for political bickering. Many athletes scheduled to take part in the Olympics were unhappy at missing the opportunity to compete directly against their counterparts from Russia. Others claimed that without the Soviets the level of competition would be greatly reduced.

Although Russia and most of her allies did not compete, the People's Republic of China was there for the first time since 1952. Communist nations like Rumania and Yugoslavia became crowd favorites, and a record number of African nations competed, so there was some balm to soothe the loss of the Soviets. Despite what seemed like a major setback, the games went on.

In fact, they were an Olympics of record achievements by gifted athletes from all over the world and an Olympics of inspirational stories. Greg Barton of the United States, who had been born with club feet and had undergone four major surgeries, training at dawn's light in Homer Lake, Michigan, won a bronze medal in men's kayaking. A paraplegic at age twenty-four after a motorcycle accident, thirty-nine-year-old Neroli Fairhall took part in the opening ceremonies, entering the Coliseum in a wheelchair. She later competed as a member of New Zealand's archery team. America's Jim Martinson had lost both legs in a land mine explosion in Vietnam. He competed in a wheelchair race, one of the events offered for the physically handicapped for the first time.

Of course, controversy did surface, as it had in other Olympics. Debate over South African policies and participation continued. Two other controversial incidents involved women runners.

In the marathon Gabriela Andersen-Scheiss came into the Los Angeles Coliseum after thirty runners had already finished. The hot sun bore down on her. She lurched, reeled, and swayed. It was clear that with the last 500 meters to still run, she was suffering from heat exhaustion.

Millions of television viewers and the seventy thousand spectators in the stadium watched as the Swiss runner painfully walked and slowly stumbled toward the finish line. Five agonizing minutes went by as Andersen-Scheiss completed the circuit of the stadium. Finally, she staggered over the finish line and fell into the arms of doctors, a spent, dehydrated athlete.

There were those who thought that she should have not been allowed to finish and risk permanent damage to her system. And there were those who viewed her effort as true grit. The debate over the painfully poignant sight of the struggling woman in the last throes of a marathon became a worldwide topic. The Swiss runner explained her own position: "The last two kilometers are mainly black. It always seemed longer to the finish than I thought."

Switzerland's Gabriela
Andersen-Scheiss staggering
from dehydration at the finish
of the women's marathon

In the 3,000-meter final a classic confrontation took place between Mary Decker and Zola Budd. Decker, an American, was the 1983 world champion, but injury and boycott had previously deprived her of the opportunity to compete in her speciality in the Olympics. Budd had posted exceptional times in the event prior to the games. Born in South Africa, which was banned by the IOC from the Olympics because of its racial policies, Budd became a British citizen in 1984.

Many claimed that Budd should not be allowed to compete in the Olympics because she was a native of South Africa and had received British citizenship because of her English-born grandfather. These claims revealed just how bizarre and political an Olympic atmosphere could become.

"Apartheid began before I was born and will probably only be resolved long after I die," Budd responded. "In the meantime I just want to run. I will run and race against anyone, anywhere, of any color, any time. And may the fastest win."

A packed Los Angeles Coliseum and a huge television audience watched the race between Mary Decker and Zola Budd under a late afternoon California sun. In the early laps the two women raced stride for stride, leading the field of other runners. Tension and silence pervaded the atmosphere.

They were into the fourth of the 7½ laps when Budd made her move to forge ahead of Decker. At the 1,750-meter point they collided. Silence in the stadium turned to shock. Decker lay flat on the infield; she didn't move.

Booing replaced the silence and unsettled Budd, who lost her composure and her thrust and finished the race in a

Zola Budd leading Mary Decker
by a small margin earlier in
the race before their collision

disappointing seventh place. The judges disqualified her immediately after the contest was completed.

A British appeal enabled Budd to be reinstated after viewing of videotapes taken from six different angles revealed that Budd was not at fault and had not intentionally collided with Decker. What apparently had happened was that Decker had caught Budd's heel with her foot, causing her younger opponent to almost stumble. Then Decker tripped over Budd's foot.

The incident had terrible implications. All of the highly touted goals of good sportsmanship were diminished by what happened afterward. Decker at first blamed Budd and refused to shake hands with the younger runner, who had always looked to Decker as an idol.

Overshadowed in all of the controversy over Decker and Budd was Maricica Puica of Rumania. She won the race and probably would have won it even if Budd and Decker had not had their unfortunate collision. Unfortunately, her gold medal performance was diminished by the incident involving the other two women.

Despite negative predictions and some real controversies, the games of the XXIII Olympiad were an astounding success, earning for the first time in history a massive 225-million-dollar surplus, which was set aside for young American athletes of the future.

More people viewed these games on television than had seen any other event in the history of the world. More than 6 million people, another world record, attended the games. Athletes represented approximately 140 nations and 23 sports. A total of 687 medals was awarded in 229 ceremonies. The United States had the largest athletic delegation —614 athletes participating in twenty-four sports—while tiny Andora had just 2 athletes in but one sport.

The People's Republic of China, Rumania, and Yugoslavia—three Communist nations—were favorites of the crowds. Their athletes were cheered wherever they went. The British Virgin Islands, Djibouti, Oman, Rwanda, the

Solomon Islands, Western Samoa, and Tonga were all in the Olympics for the first time in the history of those countries.

The success of the Los Angeles Olympics gave a shot in the arm to the Olympic movement, as the world waited for the 1988 Olympic Games.

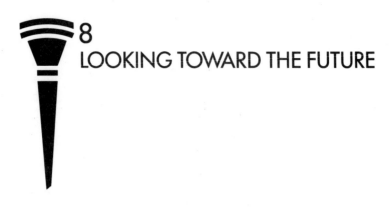

8
LOOKING TOWARD THE FUTURE

The games of the XXIV Olympiad were scheduled for Seoul, South Korea, September 17 to October 2, 1988. The split between the Communist and the free world was accentuated by the scheduling of these 1988 Summer Games in Korea, a nation divided. A history of hostility exists between North and South Korea.

Fears of a Soviet-bloc boycott of the Seoul Games were raised almost immediately after the Los Angeles Olympics ended in 1984. At that time the Communist North Koreans demanded that half of the Olympic events be staged in their country. Months of negotiations focused on this controversy in an attempt to reach a compromise.

In June 1986 Juan Antonio Samaranch, president of the International Olympics Committee (IOC), said that some events in the 1988 Olympics would be offered to North Korea under strict conditions.

Events under consideration for transfer to North Korea included cycling, table tennis, archery, and soccer. "What is important," said Samaranch, "is the gesture of South

Korea and the IOC in offering part of these Games to North Korea."

Thus, one source of controversy that figured to be part of the 1988 Summer Games seemed to be defused. However, veteran Olympic observers knew that even with the best intentions on the part of all, some type of controversy was bound to surface at Seoul.

The Olympic Games take place every four years, world politics permitting. And despite controversies, tragedies, moments of confusion, missed signals, and commercialism, the games represent a noble ideal—amateur athletes striving for perfection.

The whole world is tuned in to the grace, spectacle, and competition of the games. The world is always involved with the perfection of great athletes seeking to go faster, higher, stronger.

Memories of these dedicated young men and women—athletes racing time itself, competing against themselves, vying with their peers, and pursuing excellence—remain. There have been many who have attempted to trample on the Olympic spirit, but like the flame that symbolizes it, the games go on.

In a world lit by lightning and burdened with problems, sorrows, and terrors, it is reassuring to know that every four years an Olympic flame is also lit. The glow of that flame has often been weakened by controversy, but its glow has also brought the peoples of the world together in a true Olympic spirit.

As this book was going to press, internal unrest in South Korea, resulting in civilian protests and demonstrations and harsh governmental reprisals, raised doubts that the games could be held here. But individuals involved with the 1988 Olympics were hopeful that a compromise could be worked out and that the games would go on as scheduled.

SOME FILMS ABOUT THE OLYMPIC GAMES

Chariots of Fire (1982). Produced by The Ladd Company. Tells the story of Harold Abrahams, the champion runner, at the 1924 Olympics. This film won an Academy Award for Best Picture.

Do You Believe in Miracles? (1981). Produced by Motorola Teleprograms Inc. (MTI—the Simon and Schuster Group.) A documentary about the American hockey team's dramatic victory over the Russians in the 1980 Winter Olympics at Lake Placid, New York.

The Jesse Owens Story (1984). Produced by Paramount Pictures. This two-part television movie depicts the life of one of the greatest all-time heroes of the Olympics.

Jim Thorpe: All American (1951). (British title: *Man of Bronze*). Produced by Warner Brothers. The life story of the first international hero in sports is presented in this film.

Olympia (1936). Produced by the Nazi German government. A propaganda film about the 1936 Berlin Olympics.

Olympic Countdown (1980). Produced by ATT (American Telephone and Telegraph). A documentary that shows preparations of the American ski team, as well as other winter sports teams, for the 1980 Winter Olympics.

Walk, Don't Run (1966). Produced by Columbia Pictures. A fictional comedy that uses the 1964 Tokyo Olympics as its setting. The film stars Cary Grant.

Wee Geordie (1956). Produced by Lion International Films. This is the story of a country boy who becomes a long-distance jumper in the Melbourne Olympics.

Wilma (1977). Produced by Cappy Productions. Depicts the life of Wilma Rudolph from her childhood as a cripple to her success as an Olympic gold-medal runner.

 FURTHER READING

Chester, David. *The Olympic Games Handbook*. New York: Charles Scribner's and Sons, 1975.

Durant, John. *Highlights of the Olympics* (fifth edition). New York: Hastings House, 1977.

Epsy, Richard. *The Politics of the Olympic Games*. Berkeley, Cal.: University of California Press, 1979.

Frommer, Harvey and Frommer, Myrna. *The Games of the Twenty-Third Olympiad: Los Angeles 1984 Commemorative Book*. Salt Lake City, Utah: International Sport Publications, 1984.

Giraldi, Wolfgang. *The Olympic Games*. New York: Franklin Watts, 1972.

Guttmann, Allen. *The Games Must Go on: Avery Brundage and the Olympic Movement*. New York: Columbia University Press, 1983.

Hoberman, John M. *The Olympic Crisis: Sport, Politics, and the Moral Order*. New Rochelle, N.Y.: Caratzas, 1985.

Johnson, William O. *All That Glitters Is Not Gold*. New York: G.P. Putnam's Sons, 1972.

Kanin, David B. *A Political History of the Olympic Games.* Boulder, Col.: Westview Press, 1981.

Kieran, John. *The Story of the Olympic Games, 776 B.C. to 1976.* Philadelphia: J.B. Lippincott, 1977.

Killanin, Michael Morris and Rodda, John. *The Olympic Games 1984* (revised edition). Bridgeport, Conn.: Merrimack, 1984.

Lucas, John A. *The Modern Olympic Games.* South Brunswick, N.J.: A.S. Barnes, 1980.

MacAloon, John J. *This Great Symbol: Pierre de Coubertin and the Origins of the Modern Olympic Games.* Chicago: University of Chicago Press, 1981.

Mallon, Bill. *The Olympics: A Bibliography.* New York: Garland, 1984.

McKay, Jim. *My Wide World.* New York: Macmillan, 1973.

Poole, Lynn and Poole, Gary. *History of the Ancient Games.* New York: Astor-Honor, 1963.

Powers, John and Kaminsky, Arthur C. *One Goal: A Chronicle of the 1980 U.S. Olympic Hockey Team.* New York: Harper and Row, 1984.

Schaap, Richard. *An Illustrated History of the Olympics.* New York: Alfred A. Knopf, 1975.

Wallechinsky, David. *The Complete Book of the Olympics.* New York: Viking, 1984.

 INDEX

128